MW01015376

Task-Based Language Teaching

CAMBRIDGE LANGUAGE TEACHING LIBRARY

A series covering central issues in language teaching and learning, by authors who have expert knowledge in their field.

For a complete list of titles please visit: http://www.cambridge.org/elt/cltl

A selection of recent titles in this series:

Task-Based Language Teaching

David Nunan

University of Hong Kong

CAMBRIDGE
UNIVERSITY PRESS

CAMBRIDGE UNIVERSITY PRESS
Cambridge, New York, Melbourne, Madrid, Cape Town,
Singapore, São Paulo, Delhi, Tokyo, Mexico City

Cambridge University Press
The Edinburgh Building, Cambridge CB2 8RU, UK

www.cambridge.org
Information on this title: www.cambridge.org/9780521549479

© Cambridge University Press 2004

This publication is in copyright. Subject to statutory exception
and to the provisions of relevant collective licensing agreements,
no reproduction of any part may take place without the written
permission of Cambridge University Press.

First published 2004
7th printing 2011

Printed in the United Kingdom at the University Press, Cambridge

A catalogue record for this publication is available from the British Library

ISBN 978-0-521-84017-0 Hardback
ISBN 978-0-521-54947-9 Paperback

Cambridge University Press has no responsibility for the persistence or
accuracy of URLs for external or third-party internet websites referred to in
this publication, and does not guarantee that any content on such websites is,
or will remain, accurate or appropriate. Information regarding prices, travel
timetables and other factual information given in this work is correct at
the time of first printing but Cambridge University Press does not guarantee
the accuracy of such information thereafter.

Designing Tasks was dedicated to my young daughters Jenny and Rebecca. This work is dedicated to my grown-up daughters, Jenny and Rebecca.

Contents

Contents

Acknowledgements

Thanks to Mickey Bonin, who first encouraged me to take on this project, and to Alison Sharpe and Jane Walsh for their editorial guidance. Particular thanks to the anonymous reviewers of an earlier draft of this book who provided many insightful criticisms and suggestions. Needless to say, remaining shortcomings are mine alone.

Introduction

The purpose of the book

This book began life as the second edition to *Designing Tasks for the Communicative Classroom*. The original volume was written in the mid-1980s, and was published in 1989. At that time, task-based language teaching was beginning to arouse attention. Although it was more than a distant prospect, it was far from a mainstream concept. As with the original book, this volume is aimed at practising teachers in ELT and applied linguists (teacher trainers, language planners, and materials writers), as well as teachers in preparation.

When I began working on this volume, I quickly realized how far the field had come. It was brought home to me that I was embarking on the creation not of a second edition but of a completely new book, and that in consequence it deserved a new title.

Recently, I completed a study into the impact on policies and practices of the emergence of English as a global language (Nunan 2002, 2003). Data were collected from a range of countries in the Asia-Pacific region including Japan, Vietnam, China, Hong Kong, Taiwan, Korea and Malaysia. In interviews with teachers, teacher educators and ministry officials, and from a study of curriculum guidelines and syllabuses, 'task-based language teaching' emerged as a central concept. At the same time, I was involved in preparing a publication proposal for China on behalf of a commercial publisher. I was given a reasonable degree of latitude in putting the proposal together, but was informed that in order to be considered by the Ministry of Education it had to contain 'task-based language teaching' as its ruling rubric.

These two anecdotes illustrate the extent to which the concept has moved to the centre ground, rhetorically at least. However, it still has a long way to go to become rooted in classroom practice. In workshops and seminars in different parts of the world, I am constantly asked by teachers, 'What is task-based language teaching, and how do I make it work?' This book is an attempt to answer both parts of that question. As with *Designing Tasks*, the purpose of the book is to provide teachers with a practical introduction to task-based language teaching along with the theoretical and empirical bases that support it.

In addition to a complete revamping and updating of principles and ideas from *Designing Tasks*, I felt four areas deserved their own chapter-length treatment. These were:

- A model for task-based language teaching (TBLT) that articulated the relationship between tasks and other curricular elements.
- The empirical basis for TBLT.
- The place of a focus on form in TBLT.
- Assessing TBLT.

In order to accommodate these new chapters, chapters in the original book had to be dropped, condensed or otherwise rearranged. The structure of the present book is described below.

The structure of the book

Chapter 1 defines the notion of 'task' and illustrates the ways in which it will be used. The relationship between task-based language teaching and communicative language teaching is discussed and set within a broader curriculum framework. Ideological assumptions about the nature of language pedagogy inherent in TBLT are also discussed. In the final part of the chapter I look at the impact of the concept of TBLT on both the learner and on institutional policy and practice.

The first section of Chapter 2 introduces a framework for TBLT. The framework defines and exemplifies the key elements in the model that underlies the rest of the book. The sections that follow outline a procedure for creating an integrated syllabus around the concept of the pedagogic task and discuss issues of lesson planning and materials design. The final section summarises the key principles underpinning TBLT.

Chapter 3 looks at the key elements that constitute a task, namely, task goals, input and procedures. The chapter also deals with teacher and learner roles as well as the settings for TBLT.

One notable aspect of TBLT has been an explosion in the amount of research stimulated by the subject. The purpose of Chapter 4 is to provide a summary of this research. One area of particular interest is that of task difficulty. The research covered here provides a basis for the subsequent discussion of task grading.

The place of a focus on form in TBLT remains controversial. In Chapter 5, I examine the nature of the controversy, and spell out where I see a focus on form fitting in to a task-based instructional cycle.

Chapter 6 looks at issues and difficulties associated with the grading of tasks as well as at options for sequencing and integrating tasks into lessons or units of work. This chapter contains updated material from

Chapters 5 and 6 of the original volume, as well as a considerable amount of new content.

Task-based language teaching presents challenges in all areas of the curriculum. This is particularly true for assessment, which is coming under increasing scrutiny as it is realized that TBLT cannot be assessed according to traditional methods. In Chapter 7, I look at key concepts, issues and controversies in assessment and relate these to TBLT.

Chapter 8 is devoted to tasks and teacher development. The purpose of this chapter is to look at task construction and evaluation from the perspective of the teacher, and to provide suggestions for introducing tasks in teacher development workshops.

References

Nunan, D. 2002. English as a global language: Counting the cost. Featured presentation, TESOL International Convention, Salt Lake City, March 2002.

Nunan, D. 2003. The impact of English as a global language on educational policies and practices in the Asia-Pacific region. *TESOL Quarterly*, 37, 4, Winter 2003.

1   What is task-based language teaching?

Introduction and overview

The concept of 'task' has become an important element in syllabus design, classroom teaching and learner assessment. It underpins several significant research agendas, and it has influenced educational policy-making in both ESL and EFL settings.

Pedagogically, task-based language teaching has strengthened the following principles and practices:

- A needs-based approach to content selection.
- An emphasis on learning to communicate through interaction in the target language.
- The introduction of authentic texts into the learning situation.
- The provision of opportunities for learners to focus not only on language but also on the learning process itself.
- An enhancement of the learner's own personal experiences as important contributing elements to classroom learning.
- The linking of classroom language learning with language use outside the classroom.

In this chapter, I will map out the terrain for the rest of the book. I will firstly define 'task' and illustrate the ways in which it will be used. I will then relate it to communicative language teaching and set it within a broader curriculum framework, as well as spelling out the assumptions about pedagogy drawn on by the concept. In the final part of the chapter I will look at the impact of the concept on the learner, on one hand, and on institutional policy and practice on the other.

Defining 'task'

Before doing anything else, I need to define the central concept behind this book. In doing so, I will draw a basic distinction between what I will call real-world or target tasks, and pedagogical tasks: target tasks, as the name implies, refer to uses of language in the world beyond the classroom; pedagogical tasks are those that occur in the classroom.

Long (1985: 89) frames his approach to task-based language teaching in terms of target tasks, arguing that a target task is:

> a piece of work undertaken for oneself or for others, freely or for some reward. Thus examples of tasks include painting a fence, dressing a child, filling out a form, buying a pair of shoes, making an airline reservation, borrowing a library book, taking a driving test, typing a letter, weighing a patient, sorting letters, making a hotel reservation, writing a cheque, finding a street destination and helping someone across a road. In other words, by 'task' is meant the hundred and one things people do in everyday life, at work, at play and in between.

The first thing to notice about this definition is that it is non-technical and non-linguistic. It describes the sorts of things that the person in the street would say if asked what they were doing. (In the same way as learners, if asked why they are attending a Spanish course, are more likely to say, 'So I can make hotel reservations and buy food when I'm in Mexico,' than 'So I can master the subjunctive.') Related to this is the notion that, in contrast with most classroom language exercises, tasks have a non-linguistic outcome. Non-linguistic outcomes from Long's list above might include a painted fence, possession – however temporary – of a book, a driver's licence, a room in a hotel, etc. Another thing to notice is that some of the examples provided may not involve language use at all (it is possible to paint a fence without talking). Finally, individual tasks may be part of a larger sequence of tasks; for example the task of weighing a patient may be a sub-component of the task 'giving a medical examination'.

When they are transformed from the real world to the classroom, tasks become pedagogical in nature. Here is a definition of a pedagogical task:

> . . . an activity or action which is carried out as the result of processing or understanding language (i.e. as a response). For example, drawing a map while listening to a tape, listening to an instruction and performing a command may be referred to as tasks. Tasks may or may not involve the production of language. A task usually requires the teacher to specify what will be regarded as successful completion of the task. The use of a variety of different kinds of tasks in language teaching is said to make language teaching more communicative . . . since it provides a purpose for a classroom activity which goes beyond the practice of language for its own sake.
>
> (Richards, *et al.* 1986: 289)

In this definition, we can see that the authors take a pedagogical perspective. Tasks are defined in terms of what the learners will do in class rather than in the world outside the classroom. They also emphasize the importance of having a non-linguistic outcome.

Breen (1987: 23) offers another definition of a pedagogical task:

> . . . any structured language learning endeavour which has a particular objective, appropriate content, a specified working procedure, and a range of outcomes for those who undertake the task. 'Task' is therefore assumed to refer to a range of workplans which have the overall purposes of facilitating language learning – from the simple and brief exercise type, to more complex and lengthy activities such as group problem-solving or simulations and decision-making.

This definition is very broad, implying as it does that just about anything the learner does in the classroom qualifies as a task. It could, in fact, be used to justify any procedure at all as 'task-based' and, as such, is not particularly helpful. More circumscribed is the following from Willis (1996), cited in Willis and Willis (2001): a classroom undertaking '. . . where the target language is used by the learner for a communicative purpose (goal) in order to achieve an outcome'. Here the notion of meaning is subsumed in 'outcome'. Language in a communicative task is seen as bringing about an outcome through the exchange of meanings. (p. 173).

Skehan (1998), drawing on a number of other writers, puts forward five key characteristics of a task:

- meaning is primary
- learners are not given other people's meaning to regurgitate
- there is some sort of relationship to comparable real-world activities
- task completion has some priority
- the assessment of the task is in terms of outcome.

(See also Bygate, Skehan and Swain 2001, who argue that the way we define a task will depend to a certain extent on the purposes to which the task is used.)

Finally, Ellis (2003: 16) defines a pedagogical task in the following way:

> A task is a workplan that requires learners to process language pragmatically in order to achieve an outcome that can be evaluated in terms of whether the correct or appropriate propositional content has been conveyed. To this end, it requires them to give primary attention to meaning and to make use of their own linguistic resources, although the design of the task may predispose them to choose particular forms. A task is intended to result in language use that bears a resemblance, direct or indirect,

to the way language is used in the real world. Like other language activities, a task can engage productive or receptive, and oral or written skills and also various cognitive processes.

My own definition is that a pedagogical task is a piece of classroom work that involves learners in comprehending, manipulating, producing or interacting in the target language while their attention is focused on mobilizing their grammatical knowledge in order to express meaning, and in which the intention is to convey meaning rather than to manipulate form. The task should also have a sense of completeness, being able to stand alone as a communicative act in its own right with a beginning, a middle and an end.

While these definitions vary somewhat, they all emphasize the fact that pedagogical tasks involve communicative language use in which the user's attention is focused on meaning rather than grammatical form. This does not mean that form is not important. My own definition refers to the deployment of grammatical knowledge to express meaning, highlighting the fact that meaning and form are highly interrelated, and that grammar exists to enable the language user to express different communicative meanings. However, as Willis and Willis (2001) point out, tasks differ from grammatical exercises in that learners are free to use a range of language structures to achieve task outcomes – the forms are not specified in advance.

Reflect
Drawing on the above discussion, come up with your own definition of a pedagogical 'task'.

In the rest of the book, when I use the term 'task' I will be referring, in general, to pedagogical tasks. When the term refers specifically to target or real-world tasks, this will be indicated.

Broader curricular consideration

'Curriculum' is a large and complex concept, and the term itself is used in a number of different ways. In some contexts, it is used to refer to a particular program of study, as in 'the science curriculum' or 'the mathematics curriculum'. In other contexts, it is synonymous with 'syllabus'. Over fifty years ago, Ralph Tyler, the 'father' of modern curriculum study, proposed a 'rational' curriculum model that is developed by firstly identifying goals and objectives (syllabus), then listing, organizing and grading learning experiences (methodology), and finally finding means for determining whether the goals and objectives have been achieved (assessment and evaluation) (Tyler 1949). I have placed 'rational' in quotation marks because Tyler's approach is not necessarily more rational than previous curricular proposals. However, it was a clever rhetorical ploy because critics of the model could be accused of 'irrationality'.

Another perspective was presented in the mid-1970s by Lawrence Stenhouse who argued that at the very minimum a curriculum should offer the following:

A. *In planning*
1. Principles for the selection of content – what is to be learned and taught.
2. Principles for the development of a teaching strategy – how it is to be learned and taught.
3. Principles for the making of decisions about sequence.
4. Principles on which to diagnose the strengths and weaknesses of individual students and differentiate the general principles 1, 2 and 3 above to meet individual cases.

B. *In empirical study*
1. Principles on which to study and evaluate the progress of students.
2. Principles on which to study and evaluate the progress of teachers.
3. Guidance as to the feasibility of implementing the curriculum in varying school contexts, pupil contexts, environments and peer-group situations.
4. Information about the variability of effects in differing contexts and on different pupils and an understanding of the causes of the variations.

C. *In relation to justification*
A formulation of the intention or aim of the curriculum which is accessible to critical scrutiny.

(Stenhouse 1975: 5)

Stenhouse's perspective provided a refreshing antidote to the rather mechanistic 'rational' curriculum model because it emphasized process as well as product, elevated the teacher as an important agent of curriculum development and change, and highlighted the importance of seeing the curriculum in action. The focus on process and action make it an interesting model for those interested in task-based curriculum proposals. (I should note parenthetically that even though his model is comprehensive, it is by no means exhaustive. It says little, for example, about curriculum management and monitoring.)

My own approach to curriculum has been strongly influenced by Stenhouse. I draw a distinction between the curriculum as plan, the curriculum as action, and the curriculum as outcome. The curriculum as plan refers to the processes and products that are drawn up prior to the instructional process. These will include plans and syllabuses, text-book, and other resources, as well as assessment instruments. The curriculum as action refers to the moment-by-moment realities of the classroom as the planned curriculum is enacted. The curriculum as outcome relates to what students actually learn as a result of the instructional process.

The curriculum as plan consists of three elements: syllabus design, which is concerned with selecting, sequencing and justifying content; methodology, which is concerned with selecting, sequencing and justifying learning experiences; and assessment/evaluation, which is concerned with the selection of assessment and evaluation instruments and procedures.

This tripartite division works well enough in traditional approaches to curriculum. However, after the emergence of communicative language teaching (CLT), the distinction between syllabus design and methodology becomes more difficult to sustain. At the initial design stage, one needs to specify both the content (the ends of learning) and the tasks and learning procedures (the means to those ends) in an integrated way. This suggests a broad approach to curriculum in which concurrent consideration is given to content, procedure, and evaluation. In the next chapter, I will set out a framework for doing this.

Reflect
To what extent does the curriculum you currently use, or a curriculum with which you are familiar, contain the different dimensions described in this section? In terms of the dimensions, where are the gaps in your curriculum? What are the strengths?

Communicative language teaching

Although it is not always immediately apparent, everything we do in the classroom is underpinned by beliefs about the nature of language, the nature of the learning process and the nature of the teaching act. These days it is generally accepted that language is more than a set of grammatical rules, with attendant sets of vocabulary, to be memorized. It is a dynamic resource for creating meaning. Learning is no longer seen simply as a process of habit formation. Learners and the cognitive processes they engage in as they learn are seen as fundamentally important to the learning process. Additionally, in recent years, learning as a social process is increasingly emphasized, and sociocultural theories are beginning to be drawn on in addition to (or even in preference to) cognitive theories (see, for example, Lantolf 2000).

Another distinction that has existed in general philosophy and epistemology for many years is that between 'knowing that' and 'knowing how' (see, for example, Ryle 1949), that is, between knowing and being able to regurgitate sets of grammatical rules, and being able to deploy this grammatical knowledge to communicate effectively. In the days of audiolingualism 'knowing that' was eschewed in favour of 'knowing how'. However, now, the pursuit of both forms of knowledge are considered valid goals of language pedagogy. (This issue is taken up in greater depth in Chapter 5.)

These views underpin communicative language teaching. A great deal has been said and written about CLT in the last 30 years, and it is sometimes assumed that the approach is a unitary one, whereas in reality it consists of a family of approaches. And, as is the case with most families, not all members live harmoniously together all of the time. There are squabbles and disagreements, if not outright wars, from time to time. However, no one is willing to assert that they do not belong to the family.

The basic insight that language can be thought of as a tool for communication rather than as sets of phonological, grammatical and lexical items to be memorized led to the notion of developing different learning programs to reflect the different communicative needs of disparate groups of learners. No longer was it necessary to teach an item simply because it is 'there' in the language. A potential tourist to England should not have to take the same course as an air traffic controller in Singapore or a Columbian engineer preparing for graduate study in the United States. This insight led to the emergence of English for Specific Purposes (ESP) as an important subcomponent of language teaching, with its own approaches to curriculum development, materials design, pedagogy, testing and research.

The CLT view of language as action, was nicely captured by Savignon (1993), one of the key architects of CLT, in a state-of-the-art survey article in which she wrote:

> In Europe, during the 1970s, the language needs of a rapidly
> increasing group of immigrants and guest workers, and a rich
> British linguistic tradition that included social as well as linguistic
> context in description of language behavior, led to the Council
> of Europe development of a syllabus for learners based on

> functional–notional concepts of language use and . . . a threshold
> level of language ability was described for each of the languages of
> Europe in terms of what learners should be able to *do* with the
> language (van Ek 1975). Functions were based on assessment of
> learner needs and specified the end result, the *product*, of an
> instructional program. The term *communicative* was used to
> describe programs that used a functional–notional syllabus based
> on needs assessment, and the language for specific purposes (LSP)
> movement was launched.
>
> (Savignon 1993: 37)

While the ESP/LSP movement initially focused on the end *product* of instructional programs, CLT also forced a re-evaluation of learning *processes*. This created a dilemma for syllabus designers whose job it was to produce ordered lists of items graded according to difficulty, frequency or pedagogical convenience. With the emergence of CLT, these may no longer have been principally structural or lexical lists, but lists of functions and notions. However, lists they remained. Processes belonged to the domain of methodology. They were someone else's business. They could not be reduced to lists of items. For a time, it seemed, the syllabus designer was out of business.

One of the clearest articulations of this dilemma came from Breen. He suggested that the solution to the syllabus designer's dilemma and the resolution to the dichotomy between language product and learning process were to see them as one and the same. Rather than separating the destination and the route of language learning, they should be seen as indistinguishable. Pedagogy should:

> . . . prioritize the route itself; a focusing upon the means towards
> the learning of a new language. Here the designer would give
> priority to the changing process of learning and the potential of
> the classroom – to the psychological and social resources applied
> to a new language by learners in the classroom context. . . . a
> greater concern with capacity for communication, with the activity
> of learning a language viewed as important as the language itself,
> and with a focus upon means rather than predetermined
> objectives, all indicate priority of process over content.
>
> (Breen 1984: 52–3)

Breen is suggesting that when we place communication at the centre of the curriculum the goal of that curriculum (individuals who are capable of communicating in the target language) and the means (classroom procedures that develop this capability) begin to merge: learners learn to communicate by communicating. The ends and the means become one and the same.

Under this scenario, what happens to the product-oriented approach which emphasizes the listing of structures and the specifying of end-of-course objectives? Can a place be found for them in CLT? This issue is particularly crucial when considering the place of grammar. For some time after the rise of CLT, the status of grammar in the curriculum seemed rather uncertain. Some linguists maintained that an explicit focus on form was unnecessary, that the ability to use a second language ('knowing how') would develop automatically if learners focused on meaning in the process of completing tasks. (See, for example, Krashen 1981, 1982). In recent years, this view has come under challenge (Swain 1985, 1996; Doughty and Williams 1998), and there is now widespread acceptance that a focus on form has a place in the classroom. It is also accepted that grammar is an essential resource in making meaning (Halliday 1994; Hammond and Derewianka 2001). At present, debate centres on the extent to which a grammar syllabus should be embedded in the curriculum, some arguing that a focus on form should be an incidental activity in the communicative classroom (Long and Robinson 1998). These issues are taken up and elaborated on in Chapter 5.

Littlewood (1981) draws a distinction between a strong and a weak interpretation of CLT. The strong interpretation eschews a focus on form, while a weak interpretation acknowledges the need for such a focus. In making his case for a weak interpretation, Littlewood argues that the following skills need to be taken into consideration.

- The learner must attain as high a degree as possible of linguistic competence. That is, he must develop skill in manipulating the linguistic system, to the point where he can use it spontaneously and flexibly in order to express his intended message.
- The learner must distinguish between the forms he has mastered as part of his linguistic competence, and the communicative functions which they perform. In other words, items mastered as part of a linguistic system must also be understood as part of a communicative system.
- The learner must develop skills and strategies for using language to communicate meaning as effectively as possible in concrete situations. He must learn to use feedback to judge his success, and, if necessary, remedy failure by using different language.
- The learner must become aware of the social meaning of language forms. For many learners, this may not entail the ability to vary their own speech to suit different social circumstances, but rather the ability to use generally acceptable forms and avoid potentially offensive ones.

(Littlewood 1981: 6)

9

> **Reflect**
> What do you see as the role of grammar in the communicative
> language curriculum? Do you think that an explicit focus on
> grammar should be part of the learning experience? If so, do you
> think that the selection and grading of linguistic elements
> (grammar, vocabulary, pronunciation features, function, notions,
> etc.) should be carried out separately from the selection and
> sequencing of learning tasks?

My own position is that the curriculum needs to take account of both
means and ends, and must, in consequence, incorporate both content
and process. In the final analysis, it does not matter whether those
responsible for specifying learning tasks are called 'syllabus designers' or
'methodologists'. What matters is that both processes and outcomes are
taken care of and that there is compatibility between them. Whatever the
position taken, there is no doubt that the development of CLT has had
a profound effect on both methodology and syllabus design, and has
greatly enhanced the status of the concept of 'task' within the curriculum.

This last comment raises the question of the relationship between
communicative language teaching and task-based language teaching.
Are the terms synonymous? If so, why have two terms for the same
notion? If not, wherein lies the difference? The answer is that CLT is a
broad, philosophical approach to the language curriculum that draws on
theory and research in linguistics, anthropology, psychology and sociol-
ogy. (For a review of the theoretical and empirical roots of CLT, see
Savignon 1993). Task-based language teaching represents a realization
of this philosophy at the levels of syllabus design and methodology.
Other realizations that could fairly claim to reside within the CLT family
include content-based instruction (Brinton 2003), text-based syllabuses
(Feez 1998), problem-based learning, and immersion education
(Johnston and Swain 1997). It is also possible to find essentially
grammar-based curricula that fit comfortably within the overarching
philosophy of CLT. This is particularly true of curricula based on genre
theory and systemic-functional linguistics (Burns 2001; Hammond and
Derewianka 2001).

Alternative approaches to syllabus design

In a seminal publication in 1976, David Wilkins suggested a basic distinction between what he called 'synthetic' approaches to syllabus design

and 'analytical' approaches. All syllabuses, he suggested, fitted one or other of these approaches.

In 'synthetic' approaches, 'Different parts of the language are taught separately and step by step so that acquisition is a process of gradual accumulation of parts until the whole structure of language has been built up' (Wilkins 1976: 2). Such approaches represent the 'traditional' way of organizing the syllabus, and reflect the common-sense belief that the central role of instruction is to simplify the learning challenge for the student. One way to simplify learning is to break the content down into its constituent parts, and introduce each part separately and step by step.

A related concept that was popular in the 1960s was that of mastery learning. Having broken the subject matter down and sequenced it from easy to difficult, each item of content was introduced to the learner in a serial fashion, and a new item was not supposed to be introduced until the current item had been thoroughly mastered (thus the label 'mastery learning').

In the case of second language acquisition, however, it seemed that learners did not acquire one item perfectly one at a time. Rather they learned numerous items imperfectly, and often almost simultaneously. In addition, the learning was unstable. An item that appeared to have been acquired at one point in time seemed to have been 'unlearned' at a subsequent point in time (Ellis 1994).

Research into processes of second language acquisition would appear to offer support for the alternative offered by Wilkins to synthetic syllabuses. These are known as 'analytical' approaches because the learner is presented with holistic 'chunks' of language and is required to analyze them, or break them down into their constituent parts:

> Prior analysis of the total language system into a set of discrete pieces of language that is a necessary precondition for the adoption of a synthetic approach is largely superfluous. . . . [Such approaches] are organized in terms of the purposes for which people are learning language and the kinds of language that are necessary to meet these purposes.
>
> (Wilkins 1976: 13)

All syllabus proposals that do not depend on a prior analysis of the language belong to this second category. In addition to task-based syllabuses, we have project-based, content-based, thematic, and text-based syllabuses. Despite their differences, they all have one thing in common – they do not rely on prior analysis of the language into its discrete points.

Of course, one needs to exercise judgement when introducing learners to texts and tasks containing a wide range of language structures. This is particularly true in the early stages of the learning process.

> **Reflect**
> Make a list of the pros and cons of analytic and synthetic
> approaches to syllabus design.

Experiential learning

An important conceptual basis for task-based language teaching is experiential learning. This approach takes the learner's immediate personal
experience as the point of departure for the learning experience.
Intellectual growth occurs when learners engage in and reflect on
sequences of tasks. The active involvement of the learner is therefore
central to the approach, and a rubric that conveniently captures the
active, experiential nature of the process is 'learning by doing'. In this, it
contrasts with a 'transmission' approach to education in which the
learner acquires knowledge passively from the teacher.

Experiential learning has diverse roots in a range of disciplines from
social psychology, humanistic education, developmental education and
cognitive theory. The person who pulled these diverse, though related,
strands together was the psychologist David Kolb, who argued for an
integration of action and reflection. In his model (Kolb 1984), learners
move from what they already know and can do to the incorporation of
new knowledge and skills. They do this by making sense of some immediate experience, and then going beyond the immediate experience
through a process of reflection and transformation.

The most articulate application of experiential learning to language
teaching is provided by Kohonen (1992). In many respects, his model can
be seen as a theoretical blueprint for TBLT, as can be seen from the following list of precepts for action derived from his work.

- Encourage the transformation of knowledge within the learner rather
  than the transmission of knowledge from the teacher to the learner.
- Encourage learners to participate actively in small, collaborative
  groups (I see group and pair work as important, although I recognise
  that there are many contexts where class size makes pair and group
  work difficult).
- Embrace a holistic attitude towards subject matter rather than a static,
  atomistic and hierarchical attitude.
- Emphasize process rather than product, learning how to learn, self-
  inquiry, social and communication skills.
- Encourage self-directed rather than teacher-directed learning.
- Promote intrinsic rather than extrinsic motivation.

Kohonen highlights the fit between experiential learning and other key concepts introduced in this chapter, particularly those of learner-centredness and autonomy:

> Experiential learning theory provides the basic philosophical view of learning as part of personal growth. The goal is to enable the learner to become increasingly self-directed and responsible for his or her own learning. This process means a gradual shift of the initiative to the learner, encouraging him or her to bring in personal contributions and experiences. Instead of the teacher setting the tasks and standards of acceptable performance, the learner is increasingly in charge of his or her own learning.
>
> (Kohonen 1992: 37)

Reflect
Select two or three of these principles and brainstorm ways of implementing them in the language classroom.

Policy and practice

Fifteen years ago, task-based language teaching was still an innovation at the level of official policy and practice, although it was used as a central construct in a number of emerging research agendas (which are reviewed in Chapter 4). While there were several exciting proposals for pedagogy, few had actually been implemented.

If official documents are to be believed, TBLT has become a corner-stone of many educational institutions and ministries of education around the world. It seems to be the new orthodoxy with major publishers, most of whom claim at least one major series to be 'task-based'. In a recent study into the impact of the emergence of English as a global language on policies and practices in the Asia-Pacific region, government informants in all seven of the countries surveyed claimed that task-based teaching was a central principle driving their English language curricula (Nunan 2002, 2003). The following quote from the Hong Kong Ministry of Education is typical of the kinds of governmental pronouncements being made:[1]

> The task-based approach [upon which the curriculum is built] aims at providing opportunities for learners to experiment with

---

1 The quote refers to 'task-based language learning', but in this book I follow the conventional terminology of calling such an approach 'task-based language teaching'.

and explore both spoken and written language through learning activities that are designed to engage learners in the authentic, practical and functional use of language for meaningful purposes. Learners are encouraged to activate and use whatever language they already have in the process of completing a task. The use of tasks will also give a clear and purposeful context for the teaching and learning of grammar and other language features as well as skills. . . . All in all, the role of task-based language learning is to stimulate a natural desire in learners to improve their language competence by challenging them to complete meaningful tasks.

(CDC 1999: 41)

Whether the rhetoric matches the reality is another matter. In a study published in 1987, I reported a large gap between the rhetoric and the reality in relation to CLT. Schools that claimed to be teaching according to principles of CLT were doing nothing of the sort (Nunan 1987). I suspect the same is true today of TBLT. When asked to describe what TBLT is and how it is realized in the classroom, many people are hard pressed to do so. There are two possible interpretations for this. On the one hand it may partly reflect the fact that, as with CLT, there are numerous interpretations and orientations to the concept. That multiple perspectives and applications have developed is not necessarily a bad thing; in fact, it is probably good that the concept has the power to speak to different people in different ways. On the other hand it may simply be a case of 'old wine in new bottles': schools embracing the new 'orthodoxy' in their public pronouncements, but adhering to traditional practices in the classroom.

> **Reflect**
> If possible, obtain a copy of the curriculum guidelines from a ministry of education or official agency where you teach or where you are contemplating teaching. Does 'task-based language teaching' have a place in the curriculum? What is it?

Learner roles

So far, we have looked at task-based teaching from the perspective of the curriculum developer and the teacher. In this final section of the chapter, I would like to look at the approach from the perspective of the learner.

Learner-centredness has been an influential concept in language pedagogy for many years, and, like TBLT, it has strong links with communicative language teaching. While the learner-centred curriculum will contain similar elements to traditional curricula, a key difference is that information about learners and, where feasible, from learners will be built into all stages in the curriculum process, from initial planning, through implementation, to assessment and evaluation. Curriculum development becomes a collaborative effort between teachers and learners, since learners will be involved in decisions on content selection, methodology and evaluation (Nunan 1988). The philosophical reasons for adopting a learner-centred approach to instruction have been informed by research into learning styles and strategies (Willing 1988; Oxford 1990), as well as conceptual and empirical work in the area of learner autonomy (Benson 2002).

Breen – a frequent contributor to the literature on learner-centred teaching – has pointed out the advantages of linking learner-centredness with learning tasks. He draws attention to the frequent disparity between what the teacher intends as the outcome of a task, and what the learners actually derive from it. (We may parallel this with a similar disparity between what curriculum documents say ought to happen and what actually happens in the classroom. Learning outcomes will be influenced by learners' perceptions about what constitutes legitimate classroom activity. If the learners have been conditioned by years of instruction through a synthetic approach (see the section 'Alternative approaches to syllabus design'), they may question the legitimacy of a program based on an analytical view of language learning.

As Breen notes, outcomes will also be affected by learners' perceptions about what they should contribute to task completion, their views about the nature and demands of the task, and their definitions of the situation in which the task takes place. Additionally, we cannot know for certain how different learners are likely to carry out a task. We tend to assume that the way we look at a task will be the way learners look at it. However, there is evidence to suggest that, while we as teachers are focusing on one thing, learners are focusing on other things. We cannot be sure, then, that learners will not look for grammatical patterns when taking part in activities designed to focus them on meaning, and look for meaning in tasks designed to focus them on grammatical form.

One way of dealing with this tendency is to sensitize learners to their own learning processes by adding to the curriculum a learning strategies dimension. Eventually, it should be possible for learners to make choices about what to do and how to do it. This of course implies a major change in the roles assigned to learners and teachers. By using 'task' as a basic unit of learning, and by incorporating a focus on strategies, we open to the students the possibility of planning and monitoring their own learning, and begin to break down some of the traditional hierarchies. This is not to say that the teacher and learner will view the same task in the same way and attach the same 'meanings' to it. Nor does it absolve the teacher from the responsibility of ensuring that through an appropriate sequencing of tasks the appropriate 'formal curricula' are covered.

> **Reflect**
> Few curricula will ever be totally subject-centred or totally learner-centred. However, even in institutions in which teachers and learners have minimal input into the curriculum development process, it is possible to introduce elements of learner-centred instruction. Think about your own program, and list ways in which it could be made more learner-centred.

Conclusion

In this chapter, I have introduced and defined 'task' in relation to the general field of language curriculum design. I tried to tease out some of the conceptual differences as well as the relationships between key concepts such as curriculum, syllabus, methodology, task and exercise. Other important concepts included in the chapter were synthetic and analytical approaches to syllabus design and experiential learning. I also touched on the place of a focus on form in the task-based classroom, as well as the role of the learner and the importance of a focus on learning process as well as on language content.

In the next chapter, I will set out a framework for TBLT along with the elements that make up a task. These elements will then be elaborated on in Chapter 3.

References

Benson, P. 2002. *Teaching and Researching Autonomy in Language Learning.* London: Longman.

Breen, M. 1984. Processes in syllabus design. In C. Brumfit (ed.) *General English Syllabus Design.* Oxford: Pergamon Press.

Breen, M. 1987. Learner contributions to task design. In C. Candlin and D. Murphy (eds) *Language Learning Tasks.* Englewood Cliffs NJ: Prentice-Hall.

Brinton, D. 2003. Content-based instruction. In D. Nunan (ed.) *Practical English Language Teaching.* New York: McGraw-Hill.

Burns, A. 2001. Genre-based approaches to writing and beginning adult ESL learners. In C. Candlin and N. Mercer (eds) *English Language Teaching in its Social Context.* London: Routledge.

Bygate, M., P. Skehan and M. Swain (eds). 2001. *Researching Pedagogic Tasks: Second language learning, teaching and testing*. London: Longman.

CDC. 1999. *Syllabuses for Secondary Schools: English language secondary 1–5*. Hong Kong: Curriculum Development Council, Education Department.

Doughty, C. and J. Williams (eds). 1998. *Focus on Form in Classroom Second Language Acquisition*. Cambridge: Cambridge University Press.

Ellis, R. 1994. *The Study of Second Language Acquisition*. Oxford: Oxford University Press.

Ellis, R. 2003. *Task-Based Language Teaching and Learning*. Oxford: Oxford University Press.

Feez, S. 1998. *Text-Based Syllabus Design*. Sydney NSW: National Centre for English Language Teaching and Research, Macquarie University.

Halliday, M. A. K. 1994. *An Introduction to Functional Grammar*. Second edition. London: Arnold.

Hammond, J. and B. Derewianka. 2001. Genre. In R. Carter and D. Nunan (eds) *The Cambridge Guide to Teaching English to Speakers of Other Languages*. Cambridge: Cambridge University Press.

Johnston, K. and M. Swain (eds). 1997. *Immersion Education: International Perspectives*. Cambridge: Cambridge University Press.

Kohonen, V. 1992. Experiential language learning: Second language learning as cooperative learner education. In D. Nunan (ed.) *Collaborative Language Learning and Teaching*. Cambridge: Cambridge University Press.

Kolb, D. 1984. *Experiential Learning: Experience as the source of learning and development*. Englewood Cliffs NJ: Prentice-Hall.

Krashen, S. 1981. *Second Language Acquisition and Second Language Learning*. Oxford: Pergamon Press.

Krashen, S. 1982. *Principles and Practice in Second Language Acquisition*. Oxford: Pergamon Press.

Lantolf, J. (ed.) 2000. *Sociocultural Theory and Second Language Learning*. Oxford: Oxford University Press.

Littlewood, W. 1981. *Communicative Language Teaching: an introduction*. Cambridge: Cambridge University Press.

Long, M. 1985. A role for instruction in second language acquisition. In K. Hyltenstam and M. Pienemann (eds) *Modelling and Assessing Second Language Acquisition*. Clevedon, Avon: Multilingual Matters.

Long, M. and P. Robinson. 1998. Focus on form: Theory, research and practice. In C. Doughty and J. Williams (eds) *Focus on Form in Classroom Second Language Acquisition Research*. Cambridge: Cambridge University Press.

Nunan, D. 1987. Communicative language teaching: Making it work. *ELT Journal*, 41, 2, 136–145.

Nunan, D. 1988. *The Learner-Centred Curriculum*. Cambridge: Cambridge University Press.

Nunan, D. 2003. The impact of English as a global language on educational policies and practices in the Asia-Pacific region. *TESOL Quarterly*, 37, 4, Winter 2003.

Oxford, R. 1990. *Language Learning Strategies: What every teacher should know*. Boston: Newbury House.

Richards, J., J. Platt and H. Weber. 1986. *Longman Dictionary of Applied Linguistics*. London: Longman.

Ryle, G. 1949. *The Concept of Mind*. London: Hutchinson.

Savignon, S. 1993. Communicative language teaching: the state of the art. In S. Silberstein (ed.) *State of the Art TESOL Essays*. Alexandria VA.: TESOL.

Skehan, P. 1998. *A Cognitive Approach to Language Learning*. Oxford: Oxford University Press.

Stenhouse, L. 1975. *An Introduction to Curriculum Research and Development*. London: Heinemann.

Swain, M. 1985. Communicative competence: Some roles of comprehensible input and comprehensible output in its development. In S. Gass and C. Madden (eds) *Input in Second Language Acquisition*. Rowley Mass.: Newbury House.

Swain, M. 1996. Plenary presentation. International Language in Education Conference, University of Hong Kong, December 1996.

Tyler, R. 1949. *Basic Principles of Curriculum and Instruction*. New York: Harcourt Brace.

van Ek, J. 1975. *Systems Development in Adult Language Learning: the threshold level in a European unit credit system for modern language learning by adults*. Strasburg: Council of Europe.

Wilkins, D. 1976. *Notional Syllabuses*. Oxford: Oxford University Press.

Willing, K. 1988. *Learning Styles in Adult Migrant Education*. Sydney: NCELTR.

Willis, D. 1996. *A Framework for Task-Based Learning*. London: Longman.

Willis, D. and J. Willis. 2001. Task-based language learning. In R. Carter and D. Nunan (eds) *The Cambridge Guide to Teaching English to Speakers of Other Languages*. Cambridge: Cambridge University Press.

2 A framework for task-based language teaching

Introduction and overview

In the first section of this chapter, I introduce a framework for task-based language teaching. The framework defines and exemplifies the key elements in the model that underlies this book including real-world/target tasks, pedagogical tasks and enabling skills. The next section outlines a procedure for creating an integrated syllabus around the concept of the pedagogic task. The section that follows is devoted to materials design considerations. It provides a procedure that can be used for planning lessons, materials and units of work. In the final section, the principles underlying the procedures described in the body of the chapter are laid out.

A task framework

As we saw in Chapter 1, the point of departure for task-based language teaching is real-world or target tasks. These are the hundred and one things we do with language in everyday life, from writing a poem to confirming an airline reservation to exchanging personal information with a new acquaintance. These three examples, by the way, illustrate Michael Halliday's three macrofunctions of language. Halliday argues that at a very general level, we do three things with language: we use it to exchange goods and services (this is the transactional or service macrofunction), we use it to socialize with others (this is the interpersonal or social macrofunction), and we use it for enjoyment (this is the aesthetic macrofunction).

Typically, in everyday interactions, the macrofunctions are interwoven, as in the following (invented) example:

A: Nice day.
B: That it is. What can I do for you?
A: I'd like a round-trip ticket to the airport, please.

In order to create learning opportunities in the classroom, we must transform these real-world tasks into pedagogical tasks. Such tasks can be placed on a continuum from rehearsal tasks to activation tasks.

A rehearsal task bears a clear and obvious relationship to its corresponding real-world counterpart. For example, the other day I was teaching on a course designed to help my students develop job-seeking skills. The task that my students had to complete was as follows.

Pedagogical task: rehearsal rationale

Write your resumé and exchange it with a partner. Study the positions available advertisements in the newspaper and find three that would be suitable for your partner. Then compare your choices with the actual choice made by your partner.

This task has a rehearsal rationale. If someone were to visit my classroom and ask why the students were doing this task, my reply would be something along the lines of, 'Well, I'm getting them, in the security of the classroom, to rehearse something they're going to need to do outside the classroom.'

Notice that the task has been transformed. It is not identical to the process of actually applying for a job in the world outside the classroom. In addition to the work with a partner, the students will be able to get feedback and advice from me, the teacher, as well as drawing on other resources.

Not all pedagogical tasks have such a clear and obvious relationship to the real world. Many role plays, simulations, problem-solving tasks and information exchange tasks have what I call an *activation* rationale. The task is designed not to provide learners with an opportunity to rehearse some out-of-class performance but to activate their emerging language skills. In performing such tasks, learners begin to move from reproductive language use – in which they are reproducing and manipulating language models provided by the teacher, the textbook or the tape – to creative language use in which they are recombining familiar words, structures and expressions in novel ways. I believe that it is when users begin to use language creatively that they are maximally engaged in language acquisition because they are required to draw on their emerging language skills and resources in an integrated way.

Here is an example of an activation task. It is one I observed a group of students carrying out in a secondary school classroom. It formed the basis of an extremely engaging lesson to which all students actively and animatedly contributed.

Pedagogical task: activation rationale

Work with three other students. You are on a ship that is sinking. You have to swim to a nearby island. You have a waterproof container, but can only carry 20 kilos of items in it. Decide which of the following items you will take. (Remember, you can't take more than 20 kilos with you.)

• Axe (8 kilos)	• Box of novels and magazines (3 kilos)
• Cans of food (500 grams each)	• Packets of sugar, flour, rice,powdered milk, coffee, tea (each packet weighs 500 grams)
• Bottles of water (1.5 kilos each)	• Medical kit (2 kilos)
• Short-wave radio (12 kilos)	• Portable CD player and CDs (4 kilos)
• Firelighting kits (500 grams each)	• Rope (6 kilos)
• Notebook computer (3.5 kilos)	• Waterproof sheets of fabric (3 kilos each)

This task, which worked very well, does not have a rehearsal rationale in that the teacher was not expecting the students to be shipwrecked in the foreseeable future. The aim of the task was to encourage students to activate a range of language functions and structures including making suggestions, agreeing, disagreeing, talking about quantity, how much/ how many, wh-questions, etc. (It is worth noting, however, that learners are not constrained to using a particular set of lexical and grammatical resources. They are free to use any linguistic means at their disposal to complete the task.)

One interpretation of TBLT is that communicative involvement in pedagogical tasks of the kind described and illustrated above is the necessary and sufficient condition of successful second language acquisition. This 'strong' interpretation has it that language acquisition is a subconscious process in which the conscious teaching of grammar is unnecessary: 'Language is best taught when it is being used to transmit messages, not when it is explicitly taught for conscious learning' (Krashen and Terrell 1983: 55).

The argument by proponents of a 'strong' interpretation of TBLT is that the classroom should attempt to simulate natural processes of acquisition, and that form-focused exercises are unnecessary. Elsewhere, Krashen (see, for example, Krashen 1981, 1982) argues that there *is* a role for grammar, but that this role is to provide affective support to the learner – in other words it makes them feel better because, for most learners, a focus on form is what language learning is all about, but it does not fuel the acquisition process. In fact, Krashen and Terrell argue that even speaking is unnecessary for acquisition: 'We acquire from what we hear (or read), not from what we say.' (p. 56). The role of a focus on form remains controversial, as we shall see in Chapter 5.

My own view is that language classrooms are unnatural by design, and that they exist precisely to provide for learners the kinds of practice opportunities that do not exist outside the classroom. Learners, particularly those in the early stages of the learning process, can benefit from a focus on form (Doughty and Williams 1998; Long 1985; Long and Robinson 1998), and learners should not be expected to generate language that has not been made accessible to them in some way. In fact, what is needed is a pedagogy that reveals to learners systematic interrelationships between form, meaning and use (Larsen-Freeman 2001).

In the TBLT framework presented here, form-focused work is presented in the form of enabling skills, so called because they are designed to develop skills and knowledge that will ultimately facilitate the process of authentic communication. In the framework, enabling skills are of two kinds: *language exercises* and *communicative activities*. (See Kumaravadivelu 1991, 1993 for elaboration.)

Language exercises come in many shapes and forms and can focus on lexical, phonological or grammatical systems. Here are examples of lexically and grammatically focused language exercises:

⤅

Language exercise: lexical focus

A Complete the word map with jobs from the list.

architect, receptionist, company director, flight attendant, supervisor, engineer, salesperson, secretary, professor, sales manager, security guard, word processor

Professionals	**Service occupations**
architect	flight attendant
……………..	……………..
……………..	……………..
……………..	……………..
……………..	……………..

JOBS

Management positions	**Office work**
company director	receptionist
……………..	……………..
……………..	……………..
……………..	……………..
……………..	……………..

B Add two jobs to each category. Then compare with a partner.

(Richards 1997: 8)

Language exercise: grammatical focus

A Complete the conversation. Then practise with a partner.

A. What ………… you …………?
B. I'm a student. I study business.
A. And ………… do you ………… to school?
B. I ………… to Jefferson College.
A. ………… do you like your classes?
B. I ………… them a lot.

(Richards 1997: 8)

The essential difference between these practice opportunities and those afforded by pedagogical tasks has to do with outcomes. In each case above, success will be determined in linguistic terms: 'Did the learners get the language right?' In pedagogical tasks, however, there is an outcome that transcends language: 'Did the learners select the correct article of clothing according to the weather forecast?' 'Did they manage to get from the hotel to the bank?' 'Did they select food and drink items for a class party that were appropriate and within their budget?'

A framework for task-based language teaching

Communicative activities represent a kind of 'half-way house' between language exercises and pedagogical tasks. They are similar to language exercises in that they provide manipulative practice of a restricted set of language items. They resemble pedagogical tasks in that they have an element of meaningful communication. In the example that follows, students are manipulating the forms 'Have you ever . . .?', 'Yes, I have' and 'No, I haven't.' However, there is also an element of authentic communication because, presumably, they can not be absolutely sure of how their interlocutors are going to respond.

Communicative activity

Look at the survey chart and add three more items to the list. Now, go around the class and collect as many names as you can.

Find someone who has . . .	Name
. . . driven a racing car	
. . . been to a Grand Prix race	
. . . played squash	
. . . run a marathon	
. . . had music lessons	
. . . ridden a motorcycle	
. . . flown an airplane	
. . . been to a bullfight	
. . . been scuba diving	
. . . played tennis	

(Nunan 1995: 96)

These then are the basic building blocks of TBLT. After a discussion of syllabus design considerations, we shall look at how these elements can be combined to form units of work. The framework described in this section is represented diagrammatically on the next page.

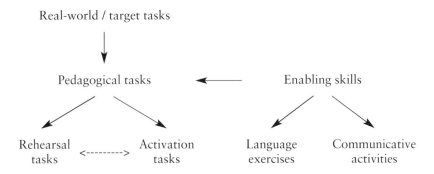

A framework for TBLT

> **Reflect**
> Find examples of these different task, activity and exercise types in
> a textbook you are currently using or one with which you are
> familiar. How are they combined?

Syllabus design considerations

One of the potential problems with a task-based program is that it may
consist of a seemingly random collection of tasks with nothing to tie
them together. In my own work, I tie tasks together in two ways. In terms
of units of work or lessons, they are tied together through the principle
of 'task chaining'. At a broader syllabus level, they are tied together
topically/thematically, through the macrofunctions, microfunctions and
grammatical elements they express. I will explore the principle of task
chaining in the next section. In this section I will look at broader syllabus design consideration.

A framework for task-based language teaching

Consider the following tasks:

1. Look at the map with your partner. You are at the hotel. Ask your partner for directions to the bank.
2. You are having a party. Tell your partner how to get from the school to your home.

Syllabus design considerations: Example 1

Tasks	Macrofunctions	Microfunctions	Grammar
Look at the map with your partner. You are at the hotel. Ask your partner for directions to the bank.	Exchanging goods and services	Asking for and giving directions	Wh-questions Yes/no questions Imperatives
You are having a party. Tell your partner how to get from the school to your home.			

These are both underpinned by the same macrofunction (exchanging goods and services), the same microfunction (asking for and giving directions) and the same grammatical elements (among others, wh-questions and imperatives).

Example 2 provides a different set of tasks realizing the same macrofunction of 'exchanging goods and services'. But here the three tasks have different microfunctions. One of the grammatical items, 'yes/no questions' is recycled from example 1.

Syllabus design considerations: Example 2

Tasks	Macrofunctions	Microfunctions	Grammar
Role play. You are in a clothing store and have $150 to spend. Your partner is the sales assistant. Look at the clothing items on the worksheet. Find out the prices and decide what to buy.	Exchanging goods and services	Asking about and stating prices	How much?/ how many? Yes/no questions
Listen to the automated ticketing service for 'What's on around town this weekend'. Make a list of movies and concerts and how much they cost. Work with three other students and decide where to go.			
Look at a set of 'to let' ads, and decide with three other students on the most suitable place to rent.			

The third example illustrates the second macrofunction, that of social-izing. The microfunction and two of the grammar items are new but, again, yes/no questions are used.

Syllabus design considerations: Example 3

Tasks	Macrofunctions	Microfunctions	Grammar
You are at a party. Introduce your partner to three other people.	Socializing	Exchanging personal information	Stative verbs Demonstrative: this Yes/no questions
Role play. You and a friend have started at a new school. Circulate and find out about your classmates.			

These considerations can all be pulled together and integrated by taking a non-linguistic organizing principle such as topics or themes and a content-based approach in which other subjects on the school curriculum, for example science, maths or geography, provide the content.

The table on p. 29 illustrates how a theme such as 'the neighbourhood' integrates several tasks which are underpinned by a range of linguistic elements.

Theme: The neighbourhood

Tasks	Macrofunctions	Microfunctions	Grammar
Look at the map with your partner. You are at the hotel. Ask your partner for directions to the bank.	Exchanging goods and services	Asking for and giving directions	Wh-questions Yes/no questions Imperatives
You are having a party. Tell your partner how to get from the school to your home.	Exchanging goods and services	Asking for and giving directions	Wh-questions Yes/no questions Imperatives
You've decided to move to a new suburb/neighbour-hood. Make a list of the facilities and services that are important to you and then decide on the best place to live based on brochures from local councils.	Exchanging goods and services	Making comparisons	Comparisons with adjectives
You have just moved to a new neighbour-hood. Introduce yourself to your neighbours.	Socializing	Exchanging personal information	Stative verbs Demonstrative: this Yes/no questions

At this point, two questions arise. Firstly, what is the difference between a 'task' and a 'function'? Secondly, in what way does a syllabus organized according to 'task' represent an advance over a functional or even a grammatical syllabus? A related question might be: won't a syllabus organized according to tasks be disorganized according to functions and grammar? We have already seen in the boxes above that certain functional and grammatical items appear more than once.

Tasks and functions are obviously closely related. Any task will be underpinned by at least one (and sometimes several) functions. Tasks can be thought of as functions + context. They allow for functions (and grammar) to be activated in a particular communicative context.

Functions are more abstract realizations than tasks of the things we do with language.

In a program based on a synthetic syllabus (whether this be a grammatical or functional syllabus), the learner, typically, will only get one or two 'shots' at the item in question. Synthetic syllabuses, sharing as they do 'a static target language product orientation', have other problems as well.

> Syllabus content is ultimately based on an analysis of the language to be learned, whether this be overt, as in the case of structure, word, notion or function, or covert, as has usually been the case with situation and topic. . . . it is assumed that the unit, or teaching point, which is presented will be what is learned and that it is efficient to organize and present material in an isolating fashion. SLA research offers no evidence to suggest that any of these synthetic units are meaningful acquisition units, that they are (or even can be) acquired separately, singly, in linear fashion, or that they can be learned prior to and separate from language use. In fact, the same literature provides overwhelming evidence against all those tacit assumptions.
>
> (Long and Crookes 1993: 26–7)

In contrast with synthetic syllabuses, a task-based syllabus allows for a great deal of naturalistic recycling. In a task-based syllabus, grammatical and functional items will reappear numerous times in a diverse range of contexts. This would appear to be healthy for second language acquisition because it allows learners to 'restructure' and develop an elaborated understanding of the item in question. It is therefore consistent with an 'organic' view of acquisition in which numerous items are acquired simultaneously, albeit imperfectly.

From research, we know that if we test a learner's ability to use a particular grammatical form several times over a period of time their accuracy rates will vary. Their mastery of the structure will not increase in a linear fashion from zero to native-like mastery. At times their ability will stabilize. At other times they will appear to get worse, not better. That is because, as Long and Crookes have pointed out, linguistic items are not isolated entities. Rather, any given item is affected by, and will affect, numerous others. As Rutherford (1987) has argued, language acquisition is an organic process and, in acquiring a language, learners go through a kind of linguistic metamorphosis. Task-based learning exploits this process and allows the learner to 'grow' into the language (Nunan 1999).

> **Reflect**
> Select one or two pedagogical tasks and elaborate them in terms of
> macrofunctions, microfunctions and grammatical exponents.

Developing units of work

In the preceding section, we looked at broader syllabus design issues. In
this section, I would like to describe how we can develop instructional
sequences around tasks. Consider the following target task taken from
example 2 in the preceding section:

**Look at a set of 'to let' ads, and decide with three other students on the
most suitable place to rent.**

With a group of pre-intermediate level students, how can we create a
linked sequence of enabling exercises and activities that will prepare
learners to carry out the task? I would like to propose a six-step procedure, and this is set out below.

Step 1: Schema building

The first step is to develop a number of schema-building exercises that
will serve to introduce the topic, set the context for the task, and introduce some of the key vocabulary and expressions that the students will
need in order to complete the task. For example, students may be given
a number of newspaper advertisements for renting accommodation of
different kinds such as a house, a two-bedroom apartment, a studio
apartment, etc., a list of key words and a series of photos of families,
couples and single people. They have to identify key words, some written
as abbreviations, and then match the people in the photos to the most
suitable accommodation.

Step 2: Controlled practice

The next step is to provide students with controlled practice in using the
target language vocabulary, structures and functions. One way of doing this
would be to present learners with a brief conversation between two people
discussing accommodation options relating to one of the advertisements
that they studied in step 1. They could be asked to listen to and read the
conversation, and then practise it in pairs. In this way, early in the instructional cycle, they would get to see, hear and practise the target language for
the unit of work. This type of controlled practice extends the scaffolded

31

learning that was initiated in step 1. They could then be asked to practise variations on this conversation model using other advertisements in step 1 as cues. Finally, they could be asked to cover up the conversational model and practice again, using only the cues from step 1, and without the requirement that they follow the conversational model word for word.

At this point, the lesson might be indistinguishable from a more traditional audiolingual or situational lesson. The difference is, however, that the learners have been introduced to the language within a communicative context. In the final part of the step, they are also beginning to develop a degree of communicative flexibility.

Step 3: Authentic listening practice

The next step involves learners in intensive listening practice. The listening texts could involve a number of native speakers inquiring about accommodation options, and the task for the learner would be to match the conversations with the advertisements from step 1. This step would expose them to authentic or simulated conversation, which could incorporate but extend the language from the model conversation in step 2.

Step 4: Focus on linguistic elements

The students now get to take part in a sequence of exercises in which the focus is on one or more linguistic elements. They might listen again to the conversations from step 3 and note the intonation contours for different question types. They could then use cue words to write questions and answers involving comparatives and superlatives: 'The two-bedroom apartment is cheaper than the three-bedroom apartment', 'Which house is closer to public transport?', 'This flat is the most spacious', etc.

Note that in a more traditional synthetic approach, this language focus work would probably occur as step 1. In the task-based procedure being presented here, it occurs relatively late in the instructional sequence. Before analyzing elements of the linguistic system, they have seen, heard and spoken the target language within a communicative context. Hopefully, this will make it easier for the learner to see the relationship between communicative meaning and linguistic form than when linguistic elements are isolated and presented out of context as is often the case in more traditional approaches.

Step 5: Provide freer practice

So far, students have been involved in what I call 'reproductive' language work; in other words, they have been working within the constraints of language models provided by the teacher and the materials. At this point, it is time for the students to engage in freer practice, where they move beyond simple manipulation. For example, working in pairs they could take part in an information gap role play in which Student A plays the part of a potential tenant and Student B plays the part of a rental agent. Student A makes a note of his or her needs and then calls the rental agent. Student B has a selection of newspaper advertisements and uses these to offer Student A suitable accommodation.

The student should be encouraged to extemporize, using whatever language they have at their disposal to complete the task. Some students may 'stick to the script', while others will take the opportunity to innovate. Those who innovate will be producing what is known as 'pushed output' (Swain 1995) because the learners will be 'pushed' by the task to the edge of their current linguistic competence. This will result in discourse that begins to draw closer to the discourse of normal conversation, exhibiting features such as the negotiation of meaning. In this process, they will create their own meanings and, at times, their own language. To begin with, this will result in idiosyncratic 'interlanguage', but over time it will approximate more and more closely to native speaker norms as learners 'grow' into the language. (See Rutherford 1987, and Nunan 1999, for an account of language acquisition as an 'organic' process.) As we shall see in Chapter 4, it has been hypothesized that such creative language work is healthy for second language acquisition (Long 1985; Martyn 1996, 2001).

Step 6: Introduce the pedagogical task

The final step in the instruction sequence is the introduction of the pedagogical task itself – in this case a small group task in which the participants have to study a set of newspaper advertisements and decide on the most suitable place to rent.

This six-step instructional sequence is summarized on pp. 34–5. When using this sequence, I sometimes at the outset show the students the final task in the sequence and ask them if they can do it. The usual response from most students is a negative one (and sometimes one of outright horror). Generally speaking, however, students find it highly motivating, having worked through the sequence, to arrive at step 6 and find that they are able to complete the task more or less successfully.

A framework for task-based language teaching

A pedagogical sequence for introducing tasks

Step 1	Example
Create a number of schema-building tasks that introduce initial vocabulary, language and context for the task.	Look at newspaper advertisements for renting accommodation. Identify key words (some written as abbreviations), and match people with accommodation.
Step 2	**Example**
Give learners controlled practice in the target language vocabulary, structures and functions.	Listen to a model conversation between two people discussing accommodation options and practise the conversation. Practise again using the same conversation model but information from the advertisements in step 1. In the final practise, try to move away from following the conversation model word for word.
Step 3	**Example**
Give learners authentic listening practice.	Listen to several native speakers inquiring about accommodation and match the conversations with newspaper ads.
Step 4	**Example**
Focus learners on linguistic elements, e.g. grammar and vocabulary.	Listen again to conversations and note intonation contours. Use cue words to write complete questions and answers involving comparatives and superlatives (cheaper, closer, most spacious, etc.).
Step 5	**Example**
Provide freer practice.	Pair work: information gap role play. Student A plays the part of a potential tenant. Make a note of needs and then call rental agent. Student B plays the part of a rental agent. Use ads to offer partner suitable accommodation.

Step 6	Example
Pedagogical task	Group work discussion and decision making task. Look at a set of advertisements and decide on the most suitable place to rent.

> **Reflect**
> Select a target task and develop your own instructional sequence using this six-step procedure as a model.

Seven principles for task-based language teaching

In this final section of the chapter, I will summarize the underlying principles that were drawn on in developing the instructional sequence outlined above.

Principle 1: Scaffolding

- Lessons and materials should provide supporting frameworks within which the learning takes place. At the beginning of the learning process, learners should not be expected to produce language that has not been introduced either explicitly or implicitly.

A basic role for an educator is to provide a supporting framework within which the learning can take place. This is particularly important in the case of analytical approaches such as TBLT in which the learners will encounter holistic 'chunks' of language that will often be beyond their current processing capacity. The 'art' of TBLT is knowing when to remove the scaffolding. If the scaffolding is removed prematurely, the learning process will 'collapse'. If it is maintained too long, the learners will not develop the independence required for autonomous language use.

Principle 2: Task dependency

- Within a lesson, one task should grow out of, and build upon, the ones that have gone before.

The task dependency principle is illustrated in the instructional sequence above which shows how each task exploits and builds on the one that has gone before. In a sense, the sequence tells a 'pedagogical' story, as learners are led step by step to the point where they are able to carry out the final pedagogical task in the sequence.

Within the task-dependency framework, a number of other principles are in operation. One of these is the receptive-to-productive principle. Here, at the beginning of the instructional cycle, learners spend a greater proportion of time engaged in receptive (listening and reading) tasks than in productive (speaking and writing) tasks. Later in the cycle, the proportion changes, and learners spend more time in productive work. The reproductive-to-creative-language principle is also used in developing chains of tasks. This principle is summarized separately below.

Principle 3: Recycling

• Recycling language maximizes opportunities for learning and activates the 'organic' learning principle.

An analytical approach to pedagogy is based on the assumption that learning is not an all-or-nothing process, that mastery learning is a misconception, and that learning is piecemeal and inherently unstable. If it is accepted that learners will not achieve one hundred per cent mastery the first time they encounter a particular linguistic item, then it follows that they need to be reintroduced to that item over a period of time. This recycling allows learners to encounter target language items in a range of different environments, both linguistic and experiential. In this way they will see how a particular item functions in conjunction with other closely related items in the linguistic 'jigsaw puzzle'. They will also see how it functions in relation to different content areas. For example, they will come to see how 'expressing likes and dislikes' and 'yes/no questions with do/does' function in a range of content areas, from the world of entertainment to the world of food.

Principle 4: Active learning

• Learners learn best by actively using the language they are learning.

In Chapter 1, I gave a brief introduction to the concept of experiential learning. A key principle behind this concept is that learners learn best through doing – through actively constructing their own knowledge rather than having it transmitted to them by the teacher. When applied to language teaching, this suggests that most class time should be devoted to opportunities for learners to use the language. These opportunities could be many and varied, from practising memorized dialogues to completing a table or chart based on some listening input. The key point, however, is that it is the learner, not the teacher, who is doing the work. This is not to suggest that there is no place at all for teacher input, explanation and so on, but that such teacher-focused work should not dominate class time.

Principle 5: Integration

- Learners should be taught in ways that make clear the relationships between linguistic form, communicative function and semantic meaning.

Until fairly recently, most approaches to language teaching were based on a synthetic approach in which the linguistic elements – the grammatical, lexical and phonological components – were taught separately. This approach was challenged in the 1980s by proponents of early versions of communicative language teaching who argued that a focus on form was unnecessary, and that all learners needed in order to acquire a language were opportunities to communicate in the language. This led to a split between proponents of form-based instruction and proponents of meaning-based instruction, with proponents of meaning-based instruction arguing that, while a mastery of grammar is fundamental to effective communication, an explicit focus on form is unnecessary. More recently, applied linguists working within the framework of systemic-functional linguistics have argued that the challenge for pedagogy is to 'reintegrate' formal and functional aspects of language, and that what is needed is a pedagogy that makes explicit to learners the systematic relationships between form, function and meaning.

Principle 6: Reproduction to creation

- Learners should be encouraged to move from reproductive to creative language use.

In reproductive tasks, learners reproduce language models provided by the teacher, the textbook or the tape. These tasks are designed to give learners mastery of form, meaning and function, and are intended to provide a basis for creative tasks. In creative tasks, learners are recombining familiar elements in novel ways. This principle can be deployed not only with students who are at intermediate levels and above but also with beginners if the instructional process is carefully sequenced.

Principle 7: Reflection

- Learners should be given opportunities to reflect on what they have learned and how well they are doing.

Becoming a reflective learner is part of learner training where the focus shifts from language content to learning processes. Strictly speaking, learning-how-to-learn does not have a more privileged place in one particular approach to pedagogy than in any other. However, I feel this reflective element has a particular affinity with task-based language teaching. TBLT introduces learners to a broad array of pedagogical undertakings, each of which is underpinned by at least one strategy. Research suggests that learners who are aware of the strategies driving their learning will be better learners. Additionally, for learners who have done most of their learning in 'traditional' classrooms, TBLT can be mystifying and even alienating, leading them to ask, 'Why are we doing this?' Adding a reflective element to teaching can help learners see the rationale for the new approach.

Reflect
Evaluate the materials or textbook you are currently using or one that you are familiar with in terms of the seven principles articulated in this section.

Conclusion

The main aim of this chapter has been to develop a framework for transforming target or real-world tasks into pedagogical tasks. I devoted the first part of the chapter to a description and exemplification of the various elements that go in to a curriculum in which the task is the basic organizing principle. This was followed by a section that sets out a procedure for integrating other elements including functions and structures. I then provided a detailed example of how an instructional sequence, integrating all of these elements, can be put together. The chapter concluded with a summary of the principles underlying the instructional sequence.

In the next chapter, we will look at the core components that go to make up a task, including goals, input data, procedures, teacher and learner roles and task settings.

References

Doughty, C. and J. Williams (eds.) 1998. *Focus on Form in Classroom Second Language Acquisition*. Cambridge: Cambridge University Press.

Halliday, M. A. K. 1985. *An Introduction to Functional Grammar*. London: Arnold.

Krashen, S. 1981. *Second Language Acquisition and Second Language Learning*. Oxford: Pergamon Press.

Krashen, S. 1982. *Principles and Practice in Second Language Acquisition*. Oxford: Pergamon Press.

Krashen, S. and T. Terrell. 1983. *The Natural Approach*. Oxford: Pergamon Press.

Kumaravadivelu, B. 1991. Language learning tasks: Teacher intention and learner interpretation. *ELT Journal*, 45, 98–117.

Kumaravadivelu, B. 1993. The name of the task and the task of naming: Methodological aspects of task-based pedagogy. In G. Crookes and S. Gass (eds) *Tasks in a Pedagogical Context*. Clevedon, Avon: Multilingual Matters.

Larsen-Freeman, D. 2001. Grammar. In R. Carter and D. Nunan (eds) *The Cambridge Guide to Teaching English to Speakers of Other Languages*. Cambridge: Cambridge University Press.

Long, M. H. 1985. A role for instruction in second language acquisition. In K. Hyltenstam and M. Pienemann (eds) *Modelling and Assessing Second Language Acquisition*. Clevedon, Avon: Multilingual Matters.

Long, M. H. and G. Crookes. 1993. Units of analysis in syllabus design: the case for task. In G. Crookes and S. Gass (eds) *Tasks in a Pedagogical Context*. Clevedon, Avon: Multilingual Matters.

Long, M. H. and P. Robinson. 1998. Focus on form: Theory, research and practice. In C. Doughty and J. Williams (eds) *Focus on Form in Classroom Second Language Acquisition*. Cambridge: Cambridge University Press.

Martyn, E. 1996. The influence of task type on the negotiation of meaning in small group work. Paper presented at the Annual Pacific Second Language Research Forum, Auckland, New Zealand.

Martyn, E. 2001. The effects of task type on negotiation of meaning in small group work. Unpublished Ph.D. dissertation. Hong Kong: University of Hong Kong.

Nunan, D. 1995. *ATLAS 4: Learning-Centered Communication. Student's book 2*. Boston: Heinle / Thomson Learning.

Nunan, D. 1999. *Second Language Teaching and Learning*. Boston: Heinle / Thomson Learning.

Richards, J. C. with J. Hull and S. Proctor. 1997. *New Interchange: Student's book 1*. Cambridge: Cambridge University Press.

Rutherford, W. 1987. *Second Language Grammar: Teaching and learning*. London: Longman.

Swain, M. 1995. Three functions of output in second language learning. In G. Cook and B. Seidlhofer (eds) *Principles and Practice in Applied Linguistics: Papers in honour of H. G. Widdowson*. Oxford: Oxford University Press.

3   Task components

Introduction and overview

In this chapter, the definition of task laid out in Chapter 1 is elaborated on, and the task framework introduced in Chapter 2 is looked at from a slightly different perspective. What I would like to do in this chapter is to explore the elements that make up a task. These are task goals, input data and learner procedures, and they are supported by teacher and learner roles and the settings in which tasks are undertaken.

Three early conceptualizations of task components are useful here. These are Shavelson and Stern (1981), Candlin (1987) and Wright (1987a).

Shavelson and Stern (1981) articulated their concept of task-based language teaching within the context of education in general, rather than TESOL in particular. Task designers, they suggest, should take into consideration the following elements:

- Content: the subject matter to be taught.
- Materials: the things that learners can observe/manipulate.
- Activities: the things that learners and teachers will be doing during a lesson.
- Goals: the teachers' general aims for the task (these are much more general and vague than objectives).
- Students: their abilities, needs and interests are important.
- Social community: the class as a whole and its sense of 'groupness'.

(Shavelson and Stern 1981: 478)

Candlin (1987), whose work was specifically referenced against language pedagogy, has a similar list. He suggests that tasks should contain input, roles, settings, actions, monitoring, outcomes and feedback. Input refers to the data presented for learners to work on. Roles specify the relationship between participants in a task. Setting refers to where the task takes place – either in the class or in an out-of-class arrangement. Actions are the procedures and sub-tasks to be performed by the learners. Monitoring refers to the supervision of the task in progress. Outcomes are the goals of the task, and feedback refers to the evaluation of the task.

Wright (1987a) is also concerned with tasks in language teaching. He argues that, minimally, tasks need to contain only two elements. These are input data, which may be provided by materials, teachers or learners, and an initiating question, which instructs learners on what to do with the data. He rejects the notion that objectives or outcomes are obligatory on the grounds that a variety of outcomes may be possible and that these might be quite different from the ones anticipated by the teacher. (In Chapter 4, we will see that the distinction between convergent tasks, which have a single intended outcome, and divergent tasks, which allow for multiple outcomes, is a significant one for task-based research.)

Wright's point about the unpredictability of outcomes is well made, and needs to be kept in mind when we consider the role of the learner in task planning and implementation. We should likewise not lose sight of the impact of setting, including social community, and feedback on tasks. However, my own belief is that *goal* is an important task element that provides direction, not only to any given task, but to the curriculum as a whole.

Drawing on the conceptualizations of Candlin, Wright and others, I propose that a minimum specification of *task* will include goals, input and procedures, and that these will be supported by roles and settings. This simple model is represented diagrammatically below.

Goals →   ← Teacher role

Input →   TASK   ← Learner role

Procedures →   ← Settings

Reflect
Can you think of any other elements that might contribute to this model of task?

Goals

'Goals' are the vague, general intentions behind any learning task. They provide a link between the task and the broader curriculum. They are more specific than Halliday's three macroskills (interpersonal, transactional and aesthetic) mentioned in the last chapter, but are more general than formal performance objectives. The answer that a teacher might give to a question from a visitor to his or her class about why learners are undertaking a particular task will often take the form of a goal statement, for example:

'I want to develop their confidence in speaking.'

'I want to develop their personal writing skills.'

'I want to encourage them to negotiate information between each other to develop their interactional skills.'

'I want to develop their study skills.'

Goals may relate to a range of general outcomes (communicative, affective or cognitive) or may directly describe teacher or learner behaviour. Another point worth noting is that goals may not always be explicitly stated, although they can usually be inferred from the task itself. Additionally, there is not always a simple one-to-one relationship between goals and tasks. In same cases, a complex task such as a simulation with several steps and sub-tasks may have more than one underlying goal.

It should be noted in passing that goals are not value-free. Embracing one set of goals will entail rejecting others. Emphasizing cognitive goals over affective ones will give a particular cast to a curriculum or program. As Richards (2001) notes, the choices we make will reflect our ideologies and beliefs about the nature of language and learning, and the purposes and functions of education.

> In developing goals for educational programs, curriculum planners draw on their understanding both of the present and long term needs of learners and of society as well as the planners' beliefs and ideologies about schools, learners and teachers. These beliefs and values provide the philosophical underpinnings for educational programs and the justification for the kinds of aims they contain. At any given time, however, a number of competing or complementary perspectives are available concerning the focus of the curriculum.
>
> (Richards 2001: 113)

One early version of a task-based curriculum, the Australian Language Levels (ALL) project, used Halliday's macroskills as the point of departure for curriculum development. The communicative goals in this curriculum suggest that language is used for:

1. Establishing and maintaining interpersonal relationships and, through this, the exchange of information, ideas, opinions, attitudes and feelings, and to get things done.
2. Acquiring information from more or less 'public' sources in the target language (e.g. books, magazines, newspapers, brochures, documents, signs, notices, films, television, slides, tapes, radio, public announcements, lectures or written reports, etc.) and using this information in some way.
3. Listening to, reading, enjoying and responding to creative and imaginative uses of the target language (e.g. stories, poems, songs, rhymes, drama) and, for certain learners, creating them themselves.

(Adapted from Clark 1987: 226)

As intimated earlier, goals may relate not just to language, but to other aspects of the learning process. The following classification, again from the ALL project, illustrates how goals can be sociocultural, process-oriented or cultural, as well as communicative.

Goal type	Example
Communicative	establish and maintain interpersonal relations and through this to exchange information, ideas, opinions, attitudes and feelings and to get things done
Sociocultural	have some understanding of the everyday life patterns of their contemporary age group in the target language speech community; this will cover their life at home, at school and at leisure
Learning-how-to-learn	to negotiate and plan their work over a certain time span, and learn how to set themselves realistic objectives and how to devise the means to attain them
Language and cultural awareness	to have some understanding of the systematic nature of language and the way it works

(Adapted from Clark 1987: 227–32)

As we have seen, a broad distinction can be drawn between English for social purposes and English for transactional purposes – that is, for obtaining goods and services (although in authentic communication, these two purposes are often interwoven). Another distinction that can be drawn is between general 'everyday' English, and English for specific purposes. Specific purpose courses can be academic or non-academic. Non-academic courses would include courses such as English for tourism. Academic courses can focus either on specific subject areas such as science and technology or law, or on more general skills for tertiary study, such as academic writing.

These distinctions can be applied to integrated skills courses or to specific skills courses. For example, a reading program can be designed to equip learners with the skills to carry out the many reading tasks that occur in everyday life, from consulting a TV program guide to reading the sports page of the afternoon newspaper. Another programme might be designed to develop the specialized reading skills needed to undertake graduate study in an English-speaking country. Given the importance of English throughout the world as a medium of tertiary instruction, it is hardly surprising that a great deal of emphasis has been placed on this second, specialized reading goal. Courses or modules for developing listening, speaking and writing can also be divided into those for general and those for academic purposes. For example, in relation to listening, a distinction could be drawn between courses for understanding the media and courses for understanding university lectures. Again, writing courses can be divided into those concerned with basic functional writing development and those aimed at more formal writing. A task-based program for developing basic functional literacy will include things such as writing notes to the school or teacher, compiling shopping lists, completing postcards and so on. Formal writing skills will include essay and report writing, writing business letters, and note-taking from lectures and books. Such formal writing skills require high levels of language ability that many native speakers never master. For foreign language users, mastery can bring prestige and economic advancement (Forey and Nunan 2002).

The most useful goal statements are those that relate to the student not the teacher, and those that are couched in terms of observable performance. That is, a statement such as, 'The learner will give a five minute presentation on a familiar topic, speaking without notes,' is preferable to 'The learner will appreciate contemporary films.' While 'appreciation' is important, it is impossible to observe, and extremely difficult to measure, as we shall see in Chapter 7 when we examine issues of assessment in the task-based curriculum.

The focus on learner performance has been an important dimension to communicative language teaching since its first appearance. For example, in Europe, the CLT movement was led by applied linguists developing conceptual frameworks for the Council of Europe. In one of the first documents to emerge from this group, it was stated that a performance-based communicative curriculum

> . . . tries to specify foreign language ability as a *skill* rather than *knowledge*. It analyzes what the learner will have to be able to *do* in the foreign language and determines only in the second place what *language-forms* (words, structures, etc.) the learners will have to be able to handle in order to *do* all that has been specified.
>
> (van Ek 1977: 5)

The most recent work coming out of the Council of Europe adheres to the performance-based approach. In the introduction to the *Common European Framework* the authors suggest that the framework

> . . . provides a common basis for the elaboration of language syllabuses, curriculum guidelines, examinations, textbooks, etc. across Europe. It describes in a comprehensive way what language learners have to learn to do in order to use a language for

communication and what knowledge and skills they have to develop so as to be able to act effectively. The description also covers the cultural context in which the language is set. The Framework also defines levels of proficiency which allow learners' progress to be measured at each stage of learning and on a life-long basis.

(Council of Europe 2001: 1)

The *Common European Framework* defines three broad levels of language use (Basic User, Independent User and Proficient User) each of which is broken down into two further levels, giving six levels in all. The table below provides global, behavioural descriptors for learners at each of these six levels.

General levels of language use

Proficient User (C2)	Can understand with ease virtually everything heard or read. Can summarize information from different spoken or written sources, reconstructing arguments and accounts in a coherent presentation. Can express him/herself spontaneously, very fluently and precisely, differentiating finer shades of meaning even in more complex situations.
Proficient User (C1)	Can understand a wide range of demanding, longer texts, and recognize implicit meaning. Can express him/herself fluently and spontaneously without much *obvious* searching for expressions. Can use language flexibly and effectively for social, academic and professional purposes. Can produce clear, well-structured, detailed text on complex subjects, showing controlled use of organizational patterns, connectors and cohesive devices.
Independent User (B2)	Can understand the main ideas of complex text on both concrete and abstract topics, including technical discussions in his/her field of specialization. Can interact with the degree of fluency and spontaneity that makes regular interaction with native speakers quite possible without strain for either party. Can produce clear, detailed text on a wide range of subjects and explain a viewpoint on a topical issue giving the advantages and disadvantages of various options.

Task components

Independent User (B1)	Can understand the main points of clear standard input on familiar matters regularly encountered in work, school, leisure etc. Can deal with most situations likely to arise whilst travelling in an area where the language is spoken. Can produce simple connected text on topics which are familiar or of personal interest. Can describe experiences and events, dreams, hopes and ambitions and briefly give reasons and explanations for opinions and plans.
Basic User (A2)	Can understand sentences and frequently used expressions related to areas of most immediate relevance (e.g. very basic personal and family information, shopping, local geography, employment). Can communicate in simple and routine tasks. Can describe in simple terms aspects of his/her background, immediate environment and matters in areas of immediate need.
Basic User (A1)	Can understand and use familiar everyday expressions and very basic phrases aimed at the satisfaction of needs of a concrete type. Can introduce him/herself and others and can ask and answer questions about personal details such as where he/she lives, people he/she knows and things he/she has. Can interact in a simple way provided the other person talks slowly and clearly and is prepared to help.

(Council of Europe 2001: 24)

In the United States, a similar orientation is adopted by the influential standards movement. One of the most comprehensive and detailed sets of content standards yet developed within the field of language education is the Pre-k-12 standards commissioned by TESOL and developed by a team of specialists working within the United States (TESOL 1997). Within this project, standards are defined as follows:

> . . . standards indicate . . . what students should know and be able to do as a result of instruction.' [They] . . . list assessable, observable activities that students may perform to show progress toward meeting the designated standard. These progress indicators represent a variety of instructional techniques that may be used by teachers to determine how well students are doing.
>
> (TESOL 1997: 16)

46

Standards are elaborated as 'Sample Progress Indicators' which set out observable behaviours that can be used to determine whether students have met the standards. From the list below, it can be seen that these are what, in the preceding chapter, were called real-world tasks. These are used as the point of departure for designing pedagogical tasks.

- obtain, complete and process application forms, such as driver's license, social security, college entrance
- express feelings through drama, poetry or song
- make an appointment
- defend and argue a position
- use prepared notes in an interview or meeting
- ask peers for their opinions, preferences and desires
- correspond with pen pals, English-speaking acquaintances, friends
- write personal essays
- make plans for social engagements
- shop in a supermarket
- engage listener's attention verbally or non-verbally
- volunteer information and respond to questions about self and family
- elicit information and ask clarification questions
- clarify and restate information as needed
- describe feelings and emotions after watching a movie
- indicate interests, opinions or preferences related to class projects
- give and ask for permission
- offer and respond to greetings, compliments, invitations, introductions and farewells
- negotiate solutions to problems, interpersonal misunderstandings and disputes
- read and write invitations and thank you letters
- use the telephone.

Reflect
Review the goals in your own curriculum or a curriculum with which you are familiar. How comprehensive are these? To what extent are they couched in performance terms?

Input

'Input' refers to the spoken, written and visual data that learners work with in the course of completing a task. Data can be provided by a teacher, a textbook or some other source. Alternatively, it can be generated by the learners themselves. Input can come from a wide range of sources, as the following inventory from Hover (1986) shows:

> letters (formal and informal), newspaper extracts, picture stories, Telecom account, driver's licence, missing person's declaration form, social security form, business cards, memo note, photographs, family tree, drawings, shopping lists, invoices, postcards, hotel brochures, passport photos, swop shop cards, street map, menu, magazine quiz, calorie counter, recipe, extract from a play, weather forecast, diary, bus timetable, notice board items, housing request form, star signs, hotel entertainment programme, tennis court booking sheet, extracts from film script, high school year book, note to a friend, seminar programme, newspaper reporter's notes, UK travel regulations, curriculum vitae, economic graphs.

This list, which is by no means exhaustive, illustrates the rich variety of resources that exist all around us. Most, with a little imagination, can be used as the basis for communicative tasks.

The list of items above was used in a set of tasks for developing listening and speaking skills. A similar range of stimulating source materials can be used for encouraging literacy skills development. Morris and Stewart-Dore (1984: 158) make the point that while it is neither necessary nor desirable to teach every possible writing style and register, the number of writing options typically offered to students can be extended by introducing the following into the classroom:

- articles from newspapers, magazines and journals
- reports to different kinds of groups
- radio and television scripts and documentaries
- puppet plays
- news stories and reports
- research reports
- short stories, poems and plays
- press releases
- bulletins and newsletters
- editorials
- progress reports and plans for future development
- publicity brochures and posters
- instructions and handbooks
- recipes
- minutes of meetings
- scripts of group negotiations
- replies to letters and other forms of correspondence
- slide/tape presentations

- caption books to accompany a visual record of an experience
- comic books for entertainment and information sharing.

The inclusion as input of such material raises the question of authenticity. 'Authenticity' in this context refers to the use of spoken and written material that has been produced for purposes of communication not for purposes of language teaching. To my mind it is not a matter of whether or not authentic materials should be used, but what combination of authentic, simulated and specially written materials provide learners with optimal learning opportunities.

Much has been written about the differences between authentic and specially written materials. Writing about spoken language, Porter and Roberts (1981) identified the following features as differentiating specially written dialogues from authentic speech.

Feature	Comment
Intonation	Speech is marked by unusually wide and frequent pitch movement
Received pronunciation	Most speakers on British ELT tapes have an RP accent which is different from that which learners will normally hear in Britain
Enunciation	Words are enunciated with excessive precision
Structural repetition	Particular structures/functions recur with obtrusive frequency
Complete sentences	Sentences are short and well formed
Distinct turn-taking	One speaker waits until the other has finished
Pace	This is typically slow
Quantity	Speakers generally say about the same amount
Attention signals	These 'uhuh's' and 'mm's' are generally missing.
Formality	Materials are biased towards standardized language; swearing and slang are rare
Limited vocabulary	Few references to specific, real-world entities and events
Too much information	Generally more explicit reference to people, objects and experiences than in real language
Mutilation	Texts are rarely marred by outside noise

Specially written materials exhibiting the characteristics identified by Porter and Roberts have always had a central place in language learning for a very good reason. By simplifying input, they make it easier for learners to process the language. By increasing the frequency of target language items, patterns and regularities are made more ostensible to learners. Slowing down the speed of speech can make it easier to understand. This is particularly valuable for beginning learners.

However, there is also value in exposing learners to authentic input. Specially written texts and dialogues do not adequately prepare learners for the challenge of coping with the language they hear and read in the real world outside the classroom – nor is that their purpose. If we want learners to comprehend aural and written language outside class, we need to provide them with structured opportunities to engage with such materials inside the classroom.

The following extracts have been taken from published course materials.

A: Hi.
B: Hello.
A: I'm Julia.
B: Nice to meet you Julia. I'm Malcolm – Malcolm Stephenson.
A: Isn't this a great party, Malcolm? I think this music's really cool.
B: Yes, it is a good party.
A: Hey! You're British, aren't you?
B: Well, yes, I am actually.
A: I was in London last year. Do you come from London?
B: No, I come from a town called Brighton – it's quite near London.
A: Oh yeah? I've been there. I went there on the same trip. We visited some sort of castle on the coast, I think. Would that be right?
B: Yes! Brighton Pavilion.

(Nunan 1995: 172)

A: So, Mark, what do you enjoy doing more than anything else?
B: Oh gosh, I think . . . let me see. I guess I'd have to say playing the banjo.
A: Playing the . . .?
B: Banjo. Yeah . . .
A: Yeah? OK. So what's your greatest ambition in life?
B: Been playing, trying to play for . . . Sorry, what?
A: Your greatest ambition (yeah) in life.
B: Um, to be as great a banjo player as Doc Boggs.
A: Doc what?
B: Doc Boggs.
A: Who on earth is Doc Boggs?
B: He's one of the greats – from Kentucky.

A: Whatever! Who do you most admire in the world and why?
B: Living, or . . .
A: Yeah.
B: Oh, um, I don't really know. I admire how Doc Boggs plays the banjo. (laughter)

(Nunan 1995: 152)

> **Reflect**
> Compare these two extracts. What differences can you discern between them? What are the advantages of both as input to learning? How would you use the second extract – the authentic text – in a language lesson?

The arguments for using authentic written texts in the classroom are similar to those advanced for using authentic spoken texts. In second (as opposed to foreign) language contexts, Brosnan *et al.* (1984) point out that the texts learners will need to read in real life are in the environment around them – at the bank, in the mailbox, on shop doors and windows, on labels, packets, etc. They do not have to be created by the teacher. Given the richness and variety of these resources, it should be possible for teachers to select authentic written texts that are appropriate to the needs, interests and proficiency levels of their students. Brosnan *et al.* (1984: 2–3) offer the following justifications for the use of these real-world resources.

- The language is natural. By simplifying language or altering it for teaching purposes (limiting structures, controlling vocabulary, etc.) we may risk making the reading task more difficult. We may, in fact, be removing clues to meaning.
- It offers the students the chance to deal with small amounts of print which, at the same time, contain complete, meaningful messages.
- It provides students with the opportunity to make use of non-linguistic clues (layout, pictures, colours, symbols, the physical setting in which it occurs) and so more easily to arrive at meaning from the printed word.
- Adults need to be able to see the immediate relevance of what they do in the classroom to what they need to do outside it, and real-life reading material treated realistically makes the connection obvious.

Brown and Menasche (1993) argue that the authentic / non-authentic distinction is an oversimplification, and that input data can be placed on a continuum from 'genuinely authentic' to non-authentic. They suggest that there are at least five distinguishable points along this continuum:

- **Genuine**: created only for the realm of real life, not for the classroom, but used in the classroom for language teaching.
- **Altered**: While there is no meaning change, the original has been altered in other ways (for example, the insertion of glosses, visual resetting, the addition of visuals).
- **Adapted**: Although created for real life, vocabulary and grammatical structures are changed to simplify the text.
- **Simulated**: Although specially written by the author for purposes of language teaching, the author tries to make it look authentic by using characteristics of genuine texts.
- **Minimal / incidental**: Created for the classroom with no attempt to make the material appear genuine.

For language programs aimed at developing academic skills, or those preparing students for further study, authentic content can be taken from subject areas in the school curriculum (Brinton 2003; Snow and Brinton 1997). Activities can be adapted from relevant academic disciplines. By reading in their intended subject areas, students will begin to develop a feel for their chosen discipline. For example, by reading science texts, learners will develop a feel for scientific discourse (i.e. the way explanations and arguments are presented by scientists working in the particular branch of the discipline in question).

Each area of specialization – science, geography, home economics, physical education, music, art and so on – has its own body of literature, which presents the content of that area in a language style of its own. Once we recognize that different bodies of knowledge have their own literature and language style, we can see that the learning implications extend beyond the school scene to the worlds of work and everyday life (see Morris and Stewart-Dore 1984: 21).

> **Reflect**
> Can you envisage any difficulties for a high school English language specialist or university instructor who is asked to help second language learners read science, mathematics or engineering texts? What can the language specialist offer that the content teacher can't offer?

Procedures

'Procedures' specifies what learners will actually do with the input that forms the point of departure for the learning task. In considering criteria for task selection (and, in the next section, we will look at what research has to say on this matter), some issues arise similar to those as we encountered when considering input.

One of these is authenticity, which we have just looked at in relation to input data. While there is widespread (although not necessarily universal) acceptance that authentic input data have a place in the classroom, less attention has been paid to procedural authenticity. Early on, Candlin and Edelhoff (1982) pointed out that the authenticity issue involves much more than simply selecting texts from outside the arena of language teaching, and that the processes brought to bear by learners on the data should also be authentic. Porter and Roberts (1981) also made the point that, while it is possible to use authentic texts in non-authentic ways (for example, turning a newspaper article into a cloze passage), this severely limits the potential of the materials as resources for language learning.

Reflect

How does this issue relate to the discussion in Chapter 2 on real-world, rehearsal and activation tasks?

In considering the task framework set out in Chapter 2, I suggested that tasks could be analyzed in terms of the extent to which they require learners to rehearse, in class, the sorts of communicative behaviours they might be expected to use in genuine communicative interactions outside the classroom. This issue of task authenticity is somewhat controversial, as can be seen from the following quotes:

> Classroom activities should parallel the 'real world' as closely as possible. Since language is a tool of communication, methods and materials should concentrate on the message, not the medium. In addition, the purposes of reading should be the same in class as they are in real life: 1) to obtain a specific fact or piece of information (scanning), 2) to obtain the general idea of the author (skimming), 3) to obtain a comprehensive understanding of reading, as in reading a textbook (thorough comprehension), or 4) to evaluate information in order to determine where it fits into our own system of beliefs (critical reading). Our students should become as critical as we are of the purposes for reading, so that they will be able to determine the proper approaches to a reading task.
>
> (Clark and Silberstein 1977: 51)

In the following quote, Widdowson argues against the notion that classroom procedures should necessarily mirror communicative performance in the real world, stating that:

> ... what is wanted is a methodology which will ... provide for communicative competence by functional investment. [Such a methodology] would engage the learners in problem-solving tasks as purposeful activities but without the rehearsal requirement that they should be realistic or 'authentic' as natural social behaviour.
>
> (Widdowson 1987: 71)

Here, Widdowson is advancing an argument in favour of a curriculum consisting exclusively of tasks with an activation rather than rehearsal rationale. (See the beginning of Chapter 2 for a discussion of the difference between these two rationales.) My own view is that both are equally valid.

All too often, discussions of authenticity in language teaching are restricted to authenticity of input data. However, in this section, I have looked at an equally important issue – that of procedural authenticity. Those procedures that attempt to replicate and rehearse in the classroom the kinds of things that learners need to do outside of the classroom have procedural authenticity. However, a case can be made for the inclusion of non-authentic procedures. Widdowson provides one rationale for such procedures above. Another rationale was provided in Chapter 2.

Another way of analyzing procedures is in terms of their focus or goal. One widely cited way of characterizing procedural goals is whether they are basically concerned with skill getting or skill using (Rivers and Temperley 1978). In skill getting, learners master phonological, lexical and grammatical forms through memorization and manipulation. In skill using, they apply these skills in communicative interaction. Proponents of audiolingualism, with its 3Ps (presentation, practice, production), assumed that skill getting should logically precede skill using. However, as we saw in Chapters 1 and 2, this assumption is overly simplistic and does not accurately reflect the complex inter-relationships between language acquisition and use. It also overlooks, or denies, the notion that learners can learn by doing.

Reflect
How does the skill-getting / skill-using distinction play out in your own classroom or a classroom that is familiar to you? Which has the greater focus? Study the following tasks. Are they designed for skill getting or skill using?

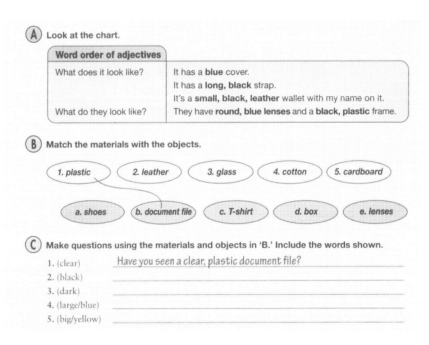

(A) Look at the chart.

Word order of adjectives	
What does it look like?	It has a **blue** cover.
	It has a **long, black** strap.
	It's a **small, black, leather** wallet with my name on it.
What do they look like?	They have **round, blue lenses** and a **black, plastic** frame.

(B) Match the materials with the objects.

1. plastic   2. leather   3. glass   4. cotton   5. cardboard

a. shoes   b. document file   c. T-shirt   d. box   e. lenses

(C) Make questions using the materials and objects in 'B.' Include the words shown.

1. (clear)   Have you seen a clear, plastic document file?
2. (black)   _____
3. (dark)   _____
4. (large/blue) _____
5. (big/yellow) _____

(Nunan 2001: 34)

Express Yourself

(A) Take out an item of yours (for example: a pen, keys, a jacket) and write a description of it on a small piece of paper.

(B) Put your descriptions in a pile. Take one. Ask questions to find out who has that item. Fill in the information in the chart. Repeat three times.

Name	Item

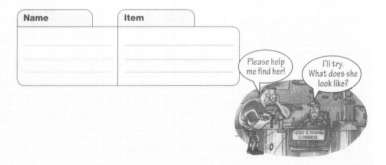

(Ibid.: 37)

A third way of analyzing learning procedures is into those that focus the learner on developing accuracy and those that focus on the development of fluency. Brumfit (1984: 51) deals with the fluency/accuracy polarity in detail:

> . . . the demand to produce work for display to the teacher in order that evaluation and feedback could be supplied conflicted directly with the demand to perform adequately in the kind of natural circumstances for which teaching was presumably a preparation. Language display for evaluation tended to lead to a concern for accuracy, monitoring, reference rules, possibly explicit knowledge, problem-solving and evidence of skill getting. In contrast, language use requires fluency, expression rules, a reliance on implicit knowledge and automatic performance. It will on occasion also require monitoring and problem-solving strategies, but these will not be the most prominent features as they tend to be in the conventional model where the student produces, the teacher corrects, and the student tries again.

Brumfit goes on to point out that accuracy and fluency are not opposites, but are complementary. However, materials and activities are often devised as if the two were in conflict, and teachers certainly adjust their behaviour depending on which one is important to them at any particular point.

Skehan (1998) also used accuracy and fluency as central constructs in his work on task-based language teaching, and added a third element – complexity. He found that different types of task generated different degrees of accuracy, fluency and complexity. I will summarize Skehan's work in the next chapter.

A final distinction that can help us to evaluate procedures has to do with the locus of control. In pattern drills and other skill-getting exercises, control usually rests with the teacher. In role plays, simulations and the like, the learner has much more control. We shall look in greater detail at teacher and learner roles later in the chapter (see also Nunan and Lamb 1996). Before that, however, I want to look at some different task types.

Task types

There are as many different task types as there are people who have written on task-based language teaching. In this section, I do not have space to deal exhaustively with them all, and so have chosen several to describe and illustrate.

One of the earliest curricular applications of TBLT to appear in the literature was the Bangalore project. In this project, three principal task types are used: information gap, reasoning gap, and opinion gap.

1. Information-gap activity, which involves a transfer of given information from one person to another – or from one form to another, or from one place to another – generally calling for the decoding or encoding of information from or into language. One example is pair work in which each member of the pair has a part of the total information (for example an incomplete picture) and attempts to convey it verbally to the other. Another example is completing a tabular representation with information available in a given piece of text. The activity often involves selection of relevant information as well, and learners may have to meet criteria of completeness and correctness in making the transfer.

2. Reasoning-gap activity, which involves deriving some new information from given information through processes of inference, deduction, practical reasoning, or a perception of relationships or patterns. One example is working out a teacher's timetable on the basis of given class timetables. Another is deciding what course of action is best (for example cheapest or quickest) for a given purpose and within given constraints. The activity necessarily involves comprehending and conveying information, as an information-gap activity, but the information to be conveyed is not identical with that initially comprehended. There is a piece of reasoning which connects the two.

3. Opinion-gap activity, which involves identifying and articulating a personal preference, feeling, or attitude in response to a given situation. One example is story completion; another is taking part in the discussion of a social issue. The activity may involve using factual information and formulating arguments to justify one's opinion, but there is no objective procedure for demonstrating outcomes as right or wrong, and no reason to expect the same outcome from different individuals or on different occasions.

(Prabhu 1987: 46–7)

Another typology that appeared at about the same time was that proposed by Pattison (1987), who sets out seven task and activity types.

Questions and answers

These activities are based on the notion of creating an information gap by letting learners make a personal and secret choice from a list of language items which all fit into a given frame (e.g. the location of a person or object). The aim is for learners to discover their classmates' secret choice. This activity can be used to practise almost any structure, function or notion.

Task components

Dialogues and role plays

These can be wholly scripted or wholly improvised. However, 'If learners are given some choice of what to say, and if there is a clear aim to be achieved by what they say in their role plays, they may participate more willingly and learn more thoroughly than when they are told to simply repeat a given dialogue in pairs'.

Matching activities

Here, the task for the learner is to recognize matching items, or to complete pairs or sets. 'Bingo', 'Happy families' and 'Split dialogues' (where learners match given phrases) are examples of matching activities.

Communication strategies

These are activities designed to encourage learners to practise communication strategies such as paraphrasing, borrowing or inventing words, using gesture, asking for feedback and simplifying.

Pictures and picture stories

Many communication activities can be stimulated through the use of pictures (e.g. spot the difference, memory test, sequencing pictures to tell a story).

Puzzles and problems

Once again, there are many different types of puzzles and problems. These require learners to 'make guesses, draw on their general knowledge and personal experience, use their imagination and test their powers of logical reasoning'.

Discussions and decisions

These require the learner to collect and share information to reach a decision (e.g. to decide which items from a list are essential to have on a desert island).

More recently, Richards (2001: 162) has proposed the following typology of pedagogical tasks:

- *jigsaw tasks* These tasks involve learners in combining different pieces of information to form a whole (e.g. three individuals or groups may have three different parts of a story and have to piece the story together).

58

- *information-gap tasks* These are tasks in which one student or group of students has one set of information and another student or group has a complementary set of information. They must negotiate and find out what the other party's information is in order to complete an activity.
- *problem-solving tasks* Students are given a problem and a set of information. They must arrive at a solution to the problem. There is generally a single resolution of the outcome.
- *decision-making tasks* Students are given a problem for which there are a number of possible outcomes and they must choose one through negotiation and discussion.
- *opinion exchange tasks* Learners engage in discussion and exchange of ideas. They do not need to reach agreement.

All of these typologies are based on an analysis of communicative language use. An alternative method of classifying tasks is to group them according to the strategies underpinning them. The following scheme proposes five different strategy types: cognitive, interpersonal, linguistic, affective and creative.

COGNITIVE	
CLASSIFYING	Putting things that are similar together in groups Example: Study a list of names and classify them into male and female
PREDICTING	Predicting what is to come in the learning process Example: Look at the unit title and objectives and predict what will be learned
INDUCING	Looking for patterns and regularities Example: Study a conversation and discover the rule for forming the simple past tense
TAKING NOTES	Writing down the important information in a text in your own words
CONCEPT MAPPING	Showing the main ideas in a text in the form of a map
INFERENCING	Using what you know to learn something new
DISCRIMINATING	Distinguishing between the main idea and supporting information

⟫→

Task components

DIAGRAMMING	Using information from a text to label a diagram
INTERPERSONAL CO-OPERATING	Sharing ideas and learning with other students Example: Work in small groups to read a text and complete a table
ROLE PLAYING	Pretending to be somebody else and using the language for the situation you are in Example: You are a reporter. Use the information from the reading to interview the writer
LINGUISTIC CONVERSATIONAL PATTERNS	Using expressions to start conversations and keep them going Example: Match formulaic expressions to situations
PRACTISING	Doing controlled exercises to improve knowledge and skills Example: Listen to a conversation, and practice it with a partner
USING CONTEXT	Using the surrounding context to guess the meaning of an unknown word, phrase, or concept
SUMMARIZING	Picking out and presenting the major points in a text in summary form
SELECTIVE LISTENING	Listening for key information without trying to understand every word Example: Listen to a conversation and identify the number of speakers
SKIMMING	Reading quickly to get a general idea of a text Example: Decide if a text is a newspaper article, a letter or an advertisement

≫→

AFFECTIVE	
PERSONALIZING	Learners share their own opinions, feelings and ideas about a subject. Example: Read a letter from a friend in need and give advice
SELF-EVALUATING	Thinking about how well you did on a learning task, and rating yourself on a scale
REFLECTING	Thinking about ways you learn best
CREATIVE	
BRAINSTORMING	Thinking of as many new words and ideas as one can Example: Work in a group and think of as many occupations as you can

(Nunan 1999)

> **Reflect**
> Review a textbook with which you are familiar and identify as many of the above strategies as you can.

The typologies introduced so far focus mainly on tasks for developing oral language skills. An early strategies-based typology for developing reading skills was proposed by Grellet (1981), who identified three main types of strategy:

- sensitizing
- improving reading speed
- from skimming to scanning.

Sensitizing is sub-categorized into:
- making inferences
- understanding relations within the sentence
- linking sentences and ideas.

From skimming to scanning includes:
- predicting
- previewing
- anticipating
- skimming
- scanning.

Grellet (1981: 12–13)

Task components

Classroom tasks exploiting these strategies include:

- ordering a sequence of pictures
- comparing texts and pictures
- matching and using illustrations
- completing a document
- mapping it out
- jigsaw reading
- reorganizing the information
- comparing several texts
- completing a document
- summarizing
- note taking.

A more recent and far more comprehensive set of reading strategies is presented by Lai (1997). Lai argues that by matching strategies, texts and reading purposes it is possible for second language readers to significantly increase both their reading speed, and also their comprehension. The strategies in her typology, along with an explanatory gloss, is set out below.

Strategy	Comment
1. Having a purpose	It is important for students to have a clear purpose and to keep in mind what they want to gain from the text.
2. Previewing	Conducting a quick survey of the text to identify the topic, the main idea, and the organization of the text.
3. Skimming	Looking quickly through the text to get a general idea of what it is about.
4. Scanning	Looking quickly through a text in order to locate specific information.
5. Clustering	Reading clusters of words as a unit.
6. Avoiding bad habits	Avoiding habits such as reading word by word.
7. Predicting	Anticipating what is to come.
8. Reading actively	Asking questions and then reading for answers.

⟫→

9. Inferring	Identifying ideas that are not explicitly stated.
10. Identifying genres	Identifying the overall organizational pattern of a text.
11. Identifying paragraph	Identifying the organizational structure of a paragraph, for example, whether it follows an inductive or deductive pattern.
12. Identifying sentence structure	Identifying the subject and main verb in complex sentences.
13. Noticing cohesive devices	Assigning correct referents to proforms,[2] and identifying the function of conjunctions.
14. Inferring unknown vocabulary	Using context as well as parts of words (e.g. prefixes, suffixes and stems) to work out the meaning of unknown words.
15. Identifying figurative language	Understanding the use of figurative language and metaphors.
16. Using background knowledge	Using what one already knows to understand new ideas.
17. Identifying style and its purpose	Understanding the writer's purpose in using different stylistic devices such as a series of short or long sentences.
18. Evaluating	Reading critically, and assessing the truth value of textual information.
19. Integrating information	Tracking ideas that are developed across the text through techniques such as highlighting and note-taking.
20. Reviewing	Looking back over a text and summarizing it.
21. Reading to present	Understanding the text fully and then presenting it to others.

(Adapted from Lai 1997)

2 Proforms are the second item of an anaphoric reference tie. They can be pronouns: 'John left the room. He was sick of the party.', or demonstratives: 'John left the room. This is because he was sick of the party.'

> **Reflect**
> Review a textbook or set of materials for teaching reading, and
> identify as many of the strategies set out above as you can.

Teacher and learner roles

'Role' refers to the part that learners and teachers are expected to play
in carrying out learning tasks as well as the social and interpersonal relationships between the participants. In this section, I will look first at
learner roles and then at teacher roles.

In their comprehensive analysis of approaches and methods in language teaching, Richards and Rodgers (1986) devote considerable attention to learner and teacher roles. They point out that a method (and, in
our case, a task) will reflect assumptions about the contributions that
learners can make to the learning process. The following table is based
on the analysis carried out by Richards and Rodgers. (Appendix A gives
further details.)

Approach	Roles
Oral Situational	learner listens to teacher and repeats; no control over content or methods
Audiolingual	learner has little control; reacts to teacher direction; passive, reactive role
Communicative	learner has an active, negotiative role; should contribute as well as receive
Total Physical Response	learner is a listener and performer; little influence over content and none over methodology
The Silent Way	learners learn through systematic analysis; must become independent and autonomous
Community Language Learning	learners are members of a social group or community; move from dependence to autonomy as learning progresses
The Natural Approach	learners play an active role and have a relatively high degree of control over content language production
Suggestopedia	learners are passive, have little control over content or methods

It is not necessary to have a detailed knowledge of these various methods to see the rich array of learner roles that they entail. These include:

- the learner is a passive recipient of outside stimuli
- the learner is an interactor and negotiator who is capable of giving as well as taking
- the learner is a listener and performer who has little control over the content of learning
- the learner is involved in a process of personal growth
- the learner is involved in a social activity, and the social and interpersonal roles of the learner cannot be divorced from psychological learning processes
- the learner must take responsibility for his or her own learning, developing autonomy and skills in learning-how-to-learn.

This last point raises the important issue of learners developing an awareness of themselves as learners, which was also raised in Chapter 2. There is growing evidence that an ability to identify one's preferred learning style, and reflect on one's own learning strategies and processes, makes one a better learner (see, for example, Oxford 1990; Reid 1995). Becoming sensitive to a range of learning processes is important in situations where task-based learning replaces more traditional forms of instruction. If learners do not appreciate the rationale behind what to them may appear a radical new way of learning, they may reject the approach.

There is some evidence to suggest that 'good' language learners share certain characteristics. The following list, adapted from Rubin and Thomson (1982), shows that the 'good' language learner is critical, reflective and autonomous. (See also Benson 2002; Nunan and Pill 2002.)

≫▸

Task components

Good language learners . . .	Implications for teachers
. . . find their own way	Help learners to discover ways of learning that work best for them, for example how they best learn vocabulary items.
. . . organize information about language	Develop ways for learners to organize what they have learned, through making notes and charts, grouping items and displaying them for easy reference.
. . . are creative	Encourage learners to experiment with different ways of creating and using language, for example with new ways of using words, playing with different arrangements of sounds and structures, inventing imaginative texts and playing language games.
. . . make their own opportunities	Facilitate active learning by getting students to interact with fellow learners and with you, asking questions, listening regularly to the language, reading different kinds of texts and practising writing.
. . . learn to live with uncertainty	Require learners to work things out for themselves using resources such as dictionaries.
. . . use mnemonics	Help learners find quick ways of recalling what they have learned, for example through rhymes, word associations, word classes, particular contexts of occurrence, experiences and personal memories.
. . . make errors work	Teach learners to live with errors and help them learn from their errors.
. . . use their linguistic knowledge	Where appropriate, help learners make comparisons with what they know about language from their mother tongue as well as building on what they have already learned in the new language.

⋙➔

. . . let the context help them	Help learners realize the relationships that exist between words, sounds and structures, developing their capacity to guess and infer meaning from the surrounding context and from their background knowledge.
. . . learn to make intelligent guesses	Develop learners' capacity to work out meanings and to guess on the basis of probabilities of occurrence.
. . . learn formalized routines	Encourage learners to memorize routines, whole phrases and idioms.
. . . learn production techniques	Help learners not to be so concerned with accuracy that they do not develop the capacity to be fluent.
. . . use different styles of speech and writing	Develop learners' ability to differentiate between styles of speech and writing, both productively and receptively.

Reflect
To what extent do the materials and tasks you use encourage or allow learners to explore and apply strategies such as these?

Learners who apply the kinds of strategies set out in the box above have adopted an active approach towards their learning. They see themselves as being in control of their own learning rather than as passive recipients of content provided by the teacher or the textbook. Many will find ways of activating their learning out of class. (See Nunan and Pill 2002 for an inventory of ways in which language can be activated out of class.)

Teacher roles and learner roles are two sides of a coin. Giving the learners a more active role in the classroom requires the teacher to adopt a different role.

Problems are likely to arise if there is a mismatch between the role perceptions of learners and teachers. According to Breen and Candlin (1980) the teacher has three main roles in the communicative classroom. The first is to act as a facilitator of the communicative process, the second is to act as a participant, and the third is to act as an observer and learner. If the learners see the teacher as someone who should be providing explicit instruction and modelling of the target language, and the teacher sees him or herself as a facilitator and guide, then conflict may arise. In such a situation the teacher may need to strike a balance between the roles that she feels appropriate and those demanded by the students.

Reflect
What role for the teacher is implicit in the following statement? Is this attitude a reasonable one, or somewhat extreme?

> The teacher as teacher is necessary only when the class is attempting to resolve a language problem, for it is only in this situation that the teacher is automatically assumed to possess more knowledge than the students. This role can be minimized if the students' attack strategies and reading skills have been effectively developed. If the task is realistic and the students have learned to adjust their reading strategies according to the task, there should be little need for teacher intervention.
>
> (Clarke and Silberstein 1977: 52).

The best way of exploring the interplay between roles and tasks is to go to where the action is: the classroom itself. The two extracts that follow were taken from tasks designed to facilitate oral interaction. However, the roles of both teacher and learners are quite different.

Extract 1

T: Stephen's Place, OK. So Myer's is on the corner. Here's the corner, OK. One corner is here and one corner is here. Two corners, OK. Can you all see the corners? Understand the corner? Can you all see the corners? This is a corner, and this is a corner here. OK? One, two. And here is the corner of the table.

S: And here?

T: Corner, yes.

S: Corner, yeah?

T: OK, Maria, where is the corner of your desk?

S: Desk?

T: Your desk.

S: This one, this one.

T: Corner? Your desk, yes, one corner.

S: Here.

T: Four corners.

S: Oh, four.

T: Yeah, four corners. Right, one . . .

S: One, two (two), three (three), four.

T: Four, four corners, yeah, on the desk. Good. OK. And where's one corner of the room? Point to one corner. Yeah, that's one corner. Yes. Another one – two, yeah. Hung, three? Francey, four. Down on the ground. Yeah, four corners.

Extract 2

S: China, my mother is a teacher and my father is a teacher. Oh, she go finish, by bicycle, er, go to . . .
S: House?
S: No house, go to . . .
S: School?
S: My mother . . .
T: Mmm
S: . . . go to her mother.
T: Oh, your grandmother.
S: My grandmother. Oh, yes, by bicycle, by bicycle, oh, is, em, accident [gestures].
T: In water?
S: In water, yeah.
T: In a river!
S: River, yeah, river. Oh, yes, um, dead.
Ss: Dead! Dead! Oh!

In extract 1, the teacher plays the role of ringmaster. He asks the questions (most of these are display questions which require the learners to provide answers which the teacher already knows. The only student-initiated interaction is on a point of vocabulary.

In the second extract, the learners have a more proactive role. The teacher here acts as a 'scaffolder' providing a supporting framework for the learner who is struggling to express herself. The extract is a nice example of what McCarthy and Walsh (2003) call the 'classroom context' mode of interaction.

In classroom context mode, opportunities for genuine, real-world-type discourse are frequent and the teacher plays a less prominent role, taking a back seat and allowing learners all the space they need. The principal role of the teacher is to listen and support the interaction, which often takes on the appearance of a casual conversation outside the classroom. (McCarthy and Walsh 2003) The danger here is that unpredictable, uncomfortable, and controversial content might arise (such as 'death' in the extract above), which could disrupt or even derail the lesson. This is one possible reason why many teachers avoid this mode of interaction, and retain a high degree of control.

Recording and reflecting on one's teaching can be illuminating (and sometimes depressing!). Here are some comments from a group of teachers who had recorded, transcribed and analyzed a recently taught task-based language lesson. The teachers were asked to reflect on what they had learned about their teaching as a result of recording and transcribing the lesson. Interestingly, all of the comments reveal attitudes towards teacher/learner roles.

- As teachers we share an anxiety about 'dominating' and so a common assumption that we are too intrusive, directive, etc.
- I need to develop skills for responding to the unexpected and to exploit this to realize the full potential of the lesson.
- There are umpteen aspects which need improving. There is also the effort of trying to respond to contradictory notions about teaching (e.g. intervention versus non-intervention).
- I had been making a conscious effort to be non-directive, but was far more directive than I had thought.
- Using small groups and changing groups can be perplexing and counter-productive, or helpful and stimulating. There is a need to plan carefully to make sure such changes are positive.
- I have come to a better realization of how much listening the teacher needs to do.
- The teacher's role in facilitating interaction is extremely important for all types of classes. How do you teach teachers this?
- I need to be more aware of the assumptions underlying my practice.
- I discovered I was over-directive and dominant.
- Not to worry about periods of silence in the classroom.
- I have a dreadful tendency to overload.
- I praise students, but it is rather automatic. There is also a lot of teacher talk in my lessons.
- I give too many instructions.
- I discovered that, while my own style is valuable, it leads me to view issues in a 'blinkered' way. I need to analyze my own and others' styles and ask why I do it that way.

> **Reflect**
> In what ways are some of the issues dealt with earlier in the chapter reflected in these comments?

Settings

'Settings' refers to the classroom arrangements specified or implied in the task. It also requires consideration of whether the task is to be carried out wholly or partly outside the classroom. A wide range of configurations is possible in the communicative classroom, although practical considerations such as class size can constrain what is possible in practice. The following diagram from Wright (1987: 58) captures the different ways in which learners might be grouped physically within the classroom.

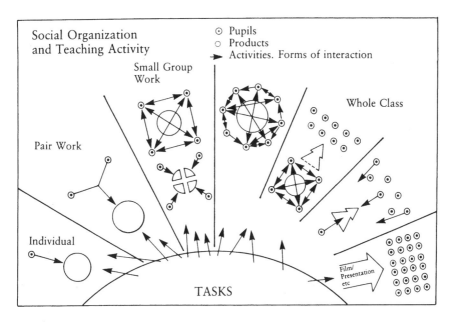

(Wright 1987: 58)

Anderson and Lynch (1988) cite second language acquisition research (which we will look at in the next chapter) to argue for an emphasis on group work in language learning.

> We might wish to use group-based work for general pedagogic reasons, such as a belief in the importance of increasing the cooperation and cohesiveness among students. Then there are more specifically language oriented arguments: classroom researchers such as Pica and Doughty (1985) have offered evidence for the positive role of group work in promoting a linguistic environment likely to assist L2 learning.
>
> (Anderson and Lynch 1988: 59)

In considering settings for task-based learning, it is useful to distinguish between 'mode' and 'environment'. Learning 'mode' refers to whether the learner is operating on an individual or a group basis. If operating on an individual basis, is the learner self-paced but teacher-directed, or entirely self-directed? If the learner is operating as part of a group, is the task mainly for whole class, small group or pair work? Each of these configurations has implications for task design.

'Environment' refers to where the learning actually takes place. It might be a conventional classroom in a school or language centre, a community class, a workplace setting, a self-access centre, or a multi-media language centre. Until comparatively recently, it was assumed that learning would take place inside a conventional classroom. However, the advent of technology, and particularly the 'anywhere/anytime' learning possibilities offered by Web-based instruction, is forcing a reconceptualization of what we mean by the concept 'classroom'.

> These changes challenge our self-concept as foreign language teachers, because much more than in the past, we are now called upon to redefine our roles as educators, since we need to mediate between the world of the classroom and the world of natural language acquisition.
>
> (Legutke 2000: 1)

There is increasing interest in the world outside the classroom as an environment for learning. Again, technology, including satellite and cable television and the Internet, and increasingly mobile workforces are facilitating this development in foreign language learning settings where instruction has traditionally been confined to the classroom. Tasks that use the community as a resource have three particular benefits:

1. they provide learners with opportunities for genuine interactions which have a real-life point to them
2. learners can adopt communicative roles which bypass the teacher as intermediary
3. they can change the in-class role relationships between teacher and pupils.

(Strevens 1987: 171)

While it is conventional wisdom that learners need to apply their language skills outside the classroom in order to progress, surprisingly little attention has been paid to learners' views on the opportunities they have for practising / learning a language outside of the classroom. In order to address this gap, Nunan and Pill (2002) investigated opportunities afforded to a group of adult learners in Hong Kong to activate their language out of class. They also investigated which opportunities were principally to obtain further practice, and which were used for authentic interaction as part of their daily lives. The study found that learners have a wide range of exposure to out-of-class English (65 different types of practice opportunities were documented), but that they find it difficult to distinguish between activities which are simply part of their lives and those that provide specific language practice.

> **Reflect**
> Consider your own approach to classroom tasks. Which student configurations do you favour? Why do you favour some ways of organizing learning over others? What opportunities are there, if any, for using the wider community as a resource for learning?

Conclusion

In this chapter, I have looked at the core task elements of goals, input and procedures, along with the supporting elements of teacher / learner roles and settings. I dealt with important constructs within TBLT, including the relationship between real-world and pedagogic tasks, text and task authenticity, and the place of learning strategies within the task-based classroom. In the next chapter, I will look at the research basis for task-based language teaching.

References

Anderson, A. and T. Lynch. 1988. *Listening*. Oxford: Oxford University Press.

Benson, P. 2002. *Teaching and Researching Autonomy in Language Learning*. London: Longman.

Breen, M. and C. Candlin. 1980. The essentials of a communicative curriculum in language teaching. *Language Learning*, 1, 2, 89–112.

Brinton, D. 2003. Content-based instruction. In D. Nunan (ed.) *Practical English Language Teaching*. New York: McGraw-Hill.

Brosnan, D., K. Brown and S. Hood. 1984. *Reading in Context*. Adelaide: National Curriculum Resource Centre.

Brown, S. and L. Menasche. 1993. Authenticity in materials design. Paper presented at the 1993 International TESOL Convention, Atlanta, Georgia. Cited in Helgeson, M. 2003. Listening. In D. Nunan (ed.) *Practical English Language Teaching*. New York: McGraw-Hill.

Brumfit, C. 1984. *Communicative Methodology in Language Teaching*. Cambridge: Cambridge University Press.

Candlin, C. 1987. Towards task-based language learning. In C. Candlin and D. Murphy (eds) *Language Learning Tasks*. Englewood Cliffs NJ: Prentice-Hall.

Candlin, C. and C. Edelhoff. 1982. *Challenges: Teacher's Book*. London: Longman.

Clark, J. 1987. *Curriculum Renewal in School Foreign Language Learning.* Oxford: Oxford University Press.

Clark, M. and S. Silberstein. 1977. Towards a realization of psycholinguistic principles in the ESL reading class. *Language Learning*, 27, 1, 48–65.

Council of Europe. 2001. *Common European Framework of Reference for Languages: Learning, teaching, assessment.* Cambridge: Cambridge University Press.

Forey, G. and D. Nunan. 2002. The role of language and culture within the accountancy workplace. In C. Barron, N. Bruce and D. Nunan (eds) *Knowledge and Discourse: Towards an ecology of language.* London: Longman.

Grellet, F. 1981. *Developing Reading Skills.* Cambridge: Cambridge University Press.

Hover, D. 1986. *Think Twice.* Cambridge: Cambridge University Press.

Lai, J. 1997. *Reading Strategies: a study guide.* Hong Kong: Chinese University of Hong Kong.

Legutke, M. 2000. Redesigning the foreign language classroom: a critical perspective on information technology (IT) and educational change. Plenary presentation, International Language in Education Conference, University of Hong Kong, Hong Kong, December 2000.

McCarthy, M. and S. Walsh. 2003. Discourse. In D. Nunan (ed.) *Practical English Language Teaching.* New York: McGraw-Hill.

Morris, A. and N. Stewart-Dore. 1984. *Learning to Learn from Text: Effective reading in the content areas.* Sydney: Addison-Wesley.

Nunan, D. 1995. *ATLAS 4: Learning-Centered Communication. Teacher's extended edition.* Boston MA: Heinle / Thomson.

Nunan, D. 1999. *Second Language Teaching and Learning.* Boston: Heinle / Thomson.

Nunan, D. 2001. *Expressions: Student book 3.* Boston MA: Heinle / Thomson.

Nunan, D. and C. Lamb. 1996. *The Self-Directed Teacher.* Cambridge: Cambridge University Press.

Nunan, D. and J. Pill. 2002. Adult learners' perceptions of out-of-class access to English. Unpublish manuscript, the English Centre, University of Hong Kong.

Oxford, R. 1990. *Language Learning Strategies: What every teacher should know.* Rowley Mass.: Newbury House.

Pattison, P. 1987. *Developing Communication Skills.* Cambridge: Cambridge University Press.

Porter, D. and J. Roberts. 1981. Authentic listening activities. *English Language Teaching Journal*, 36, 1, 37–47.

Prabhu, N. 1987. *Second Language Pedagogy: a perspective.* Oxford: Oxford University Press.

Reid, J. (ed.) 1995. *Learning styles in the ESL/EFL Classroom.* Boston MA: Heinle/Thomson.

Richards, J. C. 2001. *Curriculum Development in Language Teaching.* Cambridge: Cambridge University Press.

Richards, J. and T. Rodgers. 1986. Second edition *Approaches and Methods in Language Teaching.* Cambridge: Cambridge University Press.

Rivers, W. and M. Temperley. 1978. *A Practical Guide to the Teaching of English as a Second or Foreign Language*. New York: Oxford University Press.

Rubin, J. and I. Thomson. 1982. *How to Be a More Successful Language Learner*. Boston MA: Heinle.

Shavelson, R. and P. Stern. 1981. Research on teachers' pedagogical thoughts, judgments, decisions and behavior. *Review of Educational Research*, 51, 4, 455–98.

Skehan, P. 1998. *A Cognitive Approach to Language Learning*. Oxford: Oxford University Press.

Snow, M. A. and D. Brinton (eds). 1997. *The Content-Based Classroom: Perspectives on integrating language and content*. New York: Longman.

Strevens, P. 1987. Interaction outside the classroom: Using the community. In W. Rivers (ed.) *Interactive Language Teaching*. Cambridge: Cambridge University Press.

TESOL. 1997. ESL *Standards for Pre-K-12 Students*. Alexandria VA: TESOL.

van Ek, J. 1977. *The Threshold Level for Modern Language Learning in Schools*. London: Longman.

Widdowson, H. G. 1987. Aspects of syllabus design. In M. Tickoo (ed.) *Language Syllabuses: State of the art*. Singapore: RELC.

Wright, T. 1987a. *Roles of Teachers and Learners*. Oxford. Oxford University Press.

Wright, T. 1987b. Instructional task and discoursal outcome in the L2 classroom. In C. Candlin and D. Murphy (eds) *Language Learning Tasks*. Englewood Cliffs NJ: Prentice-Hall.

4 An empirical basis for task-based language teaching

Introduction and overview

One of the things that differentiates task-based language teaching from earlier methodological proposals is that it is supported by a rich and growing research agenda. Some of the more idiosyncratic approaches of the 1960s and 1970s may have attracted many devotees during the height of their popularity. However, little, if any, empirical research was conducted into their effectiveness. A possible exception was audiolingualism, although research carried out into the effectiveness of this approach in comparison with other methods was largely inconclusive (for a review see Bailey 1999; Nunan 2003).

In this chapter, I will focus principally on psycholinguistically oriented research, looking in particular at two influential hypotheses: the input hypothesis and the output hypothesis. I will also examine the important issue of task difficulty, exploring the different factors that make one task more difficult than another.

Chapter 5 will also review research, but will focus exclusively on research related to the place of a focus on form in task-based language teaching. It will thus be more circumscribed than the present chapter.

Early psycholinguistic models

Around the mid-1980s, a number of controversial hypotheses of language acquisition were proposed by Stephen Krashen. Although they came under concerted attack almost from the moment they were first published, to this day they remain popular, widely cited and influential, particularly in North America. They have also had a major influence on task-based language teaching, and for this reason deserve some attention.

Krashen (1981, 1982) based his hypotheses on a series of studies known as the 'morpheme order studies' (Dulay and Burt 1973, 1974). These studies investigated the acquisition of a number of key grammatical morphemes in English (these included such items as third person 's', the copula, the -ing form of the verb and the article system). These studies showed that the morphemes were acquired in pretty much the same order by learners regardless of their first language. The acquisition order was also similar regardless of the age of the learners. Finally, it was found that the order varied from the order of instruction, and that it could not be 'overturned' by instruction.

Data from these studies led Krashen to formulate four hypotheses. These are the acquisition-learning hypothesis, the natural order hypothesis, the monitor hypothesis and the input hypothesis.

The acquisition-learning hypothesis

The acquisition-learning hypothesis claims that there are two psycholinguistic processes functioning in second language acquisition. These are conscious learning and subconscious acquisition. Subconscious acquisition is similar to the process that drives first language acquisition and is activated when the individual is focused on using the language for communication. Conscious learning involves the learning about the language through rule memorization and so on. What made Krashen's view controversial was his insistence that these are two totally separate processes, that conscious learning could not 'bleed into' subconscious acquisition, and that communicative competence in a second or foreign language could only be acquired through subconscious acquisition.

> A very important point that also needs to be stated is that learning does not 'turn into' acquisition. The idea that we first learn a new rule, and eventually, through practice, acquire it, is widespread and may seem to some people intuitively obvious. This model of the acquisition process was first presented to me when I was a student of TESL, and seemed very sensible at the time. It was, I thought, exactly the way I learned languages myself.
>
> (Krashen 1982: 83)

> . . . [However] despite our feelings that internalization does occur, the theory predicts that it does not, except in a trivial way. Language acquisition . . . happens in one way, when the acquirer understands input containing a structure that the acquirer is 'due' to acquire. . . . There is no necessity for previous conscious knowledge of a rule.
>
> (Krashen 1982: 83: 4)

The implication of the acquisition-learning hypothesis for TBLT is that time in the classroom should be devoted to opportunities for subconscious acquisition rather than conscious learning. Learners should be engaged in meaning-focused, communicative tasks rather than form-focused drills and exercises. The hypothesis thus favours the 'strong' interpretation of TBLT. (My own position is that there is a place for form-focused instruction. I set out my position and give reasons for it in Chapter 5.)

The natural order hypothesis

This hypothesis follows directly from the findings of the morpheme order studies that learners appear to acquire key grammatical features of a target language in a particular order regardless of their first language and regardless of the order in which these features have been presented through formal instruction. The hypothesis states that the order is determined by a 'natural order' or 'inbuilt syllabus' that derives from the nature of the target language and not from some contrast between a learner's first language and the one he or she is attempting to acquire (Krashen does hedge his bets a little on this particular hypothesis, stating that this is a general tendency, and not every learner will acquire grammatical structures in the identical order).

The implications of the natural order hypothesis for TBLT are not immediately apparent. In fact, the findings of the morpheme order and other acquisition order studies have led in two diametrically opposite directions. One line of argument has it that we should retain a grammatically sequenced syllabus, but that the sequence should mirror the 'natural order' as revealed by research rather than the order as determined by traditional grammatical analysis. The other argument leads in the other direction, stating that if there is a natural order that cannot be changed by instruction then there is little point in trying to sequence the grammar; exposure, and opportunities to use the language will be sufficient to trigger the acquisition process. This is largely the position of the 'strong' interpreters of TBLT described in Chapter 1.

The monitor hypothesis

According to this hypothesis, conscious learning has a limited function in second language acquisition. It cannot be used to generate language, but only to monitor language that is subconsciously acquired and subsequently generated. Through monitoring, we can make changes to a piece of language, but only after it has been produced. The three conditions under which the monitor can be used successfully are:

1. the speaker or writer has enough time to exercise the monitor
2. the speaker or writer is focused on form
3. the speaker or writer knows the rule.

The implications of the monitor hypothesis are similar to those for the acquisition-learning hypothesis. To maximize opportunities for acquisition, class time should be devoted to meaning-focused tasks, and learners should be encouraged not to monitor their output.

The input hypothesis

This hypothesis is one of Krashen's most controversial. It states that we acquire languages when we understand messages (input) in the target language that are just a little beyond our current level of acquired competence. According to this hypothesis, in order for learners to progress from one stage of acquisition to the next, they need to comprehend language that includes a structure at the stage beyond that of their current level. Comprehension itself comes from the context in which the language occurs as well as from extra-linguistic information. In the early stages of the acquisition process, comprehension is aided by restricting language to the 'here and now'; in other words, by only referring to things and events that are physically present in the learner's environment.

The input hypothesis suggests that reception should precede production, and that extensive opportunities for listening and reading should precede speaking and writing, particularly in the early stages of the acquisition process.

Krashen's hypotheses generated a great deal of controversy when they were first proposed, and they remain controversial to this day. In the next section, we look at an alternative to the input hypothesis; this is a hypothesis with the rather tongue-in-cheek label of the 'output hypothesis'.

Reflect

To what extent does your own experience (a) as a language teacher and (b) as a language learner lead you to agree with / disagree with Krashen's hypotheses?

Interaction, output and the negotiation of meaning

One of the first researchers to emphasize the importance of output was Hatch (1978), who argued that we learn how to converse in a second language by having conversations. Rather than learning grammatical structures, and then deploying these in conversation, Hatch argued that interaction should come first, and that out of this interaction grammatical knowledge would develop. Ellis (1984: 95) had a similar perspective, arguing that:

> Interaction contributes to development because it is the means by which the learner is able to crack the code. This takes place when the learner can infer what is said even though the message contains linguistic items that are not yet part of his competence and when the learner can use the discourse to help him/her modify or supplement the linguistic knowledge already used in production.

In 1985, Merrill Swain, a Canadian researcher, published an eloquent assault upon the input hypothesis, proposing an alternative, the 'output hypothesis'. Swain based her hypothesis on a substantial body of research carried out in Canada into the effects of immersion and content-based education. In these programs, students receive instruction in the regular subjects in the curriculum – history, mathematics, science, etc. – through a second language and, in consequence, receive huge amounts of comprehensible input. Despite this input, the students do not acquire the levels of fluency in the language predicted by the input hypothesis.

Swain argued that, while input is necessary, it is not sufficient for acquisition; in addition to input, learners need opportunities to produce the target language. This is because production involves a different psycholinguistic process from comprehension. In comprehending an utterance in a target language, one can largely bypass the syntax and 'go for meaning'. However, in order to produce a comprehensible utterance, one has to 'syntacticize' the utterance, that is, encode it grammatically.

Long (1985) also incorporated a role for output in his model of second language acquisition, although that role is different from the way it was conceived by Swain. Long argues that linguistic conversational adjustments (which are also known as the negotiation of meaning) promote comprehensible input because such adjustments are usually triggered by an indication of non-comprehension, requiring the speaker to reformulate his or her utterance to make it more comprehensible. If comprehensible input promotes acquisition, then it follows that linguistic/conversational adjustments promote acquisition. (It should be noted that negotiation of meaning is a natural aspect of everyday conversation – so natural, in fact, that we rarely notice ourselves doing it.)

Investigators have identified a four-stage process in the negotiation of meaning. The first stage is a 'trigger' that begins the sequence. This is followed by a 'signal' that draws attention to a communication breakdown. Stage 3 is a 'response', in which the speaker attempts to repair the miscommunication. More than one response may be needed at this stage to repair the breakdown. Finally, the 'follow-up' marks the closing of the sequence (Pica *et al.* 1991).

The following examples from Martyn (2001) illustrate the four-stage procedure.

She's a loner.	Trigger
Sorry?	Signal
She stay away from others.	Response
How about the other choices then?	Follow-up

I think the ah, drugs problem, ah ah, is related to the triad society.	Trigger
Triad society?	Signal
Yes.	Response
Triad society. I'm not sure. (pause) . . . But another thing//	Follow-up

(Martyn 2001: 33)

These two extracts are examples of 'simple' or 'one signal' negotiation of meaning sequences (Ellis, Basturkmen and Loewen 2001; Shehadeh 1999). However, many negotiation of meaning sequences are longer and more complex than this. The following extract – again from Martyn – of a conversation between three people includes five signals and nine responses.

≫→

F2	That is ah, some movie or comic ah, ah, insert, insert some ah, wrong concept about death. In the comic books and movie ah many characters die, they die and then they can, ah, how to say, live again?	Trigger / Signal 1
F1	Live again.	Response 1
F2	How to say live again?	Signal 2
F3	Die and//	Response 2
F2	They die and then they relive (laughs)	Response 3
F1	What relive?	Signal 3
F3	Ah, that means . . .	Signal 4
F2	Ah, they die//	Response 4
F3	. . . they never die, you mean?	Signal 4 cont.
F2	Ya . . . (that is) (laughs)	Response 5
F1	That means they never die you mean, even if they die, there is a pretended die . . .	Signal 5
F2	Just like Christ.	Response 6
F1	. . . pretended dead?	Signal 5 cont.
F2	Just like Christ.	Response 7
F3	Just like Christ . . .	Response 8
F1	I know, I know what you mean. OK, go on.	Response 9
F3	Just like Jesus Christ, and so they think that, ah, they die and then they can, ah, live again, and so when they face a pro-, face some problems, they ah, they, they, will think of committing suicide.	Response 8 cont.
F2	Ahuh, I think we need to go to the part that discuss ah why there, why has there been such an increase in recent years, right?	Follow-up

(Martyn 2001: 34)

Martyn points out that the conversation illustrates several interesting features of a negotiation of meaning sequence.

> The trigger which opens the sequence is also a signal as F2 asks a question when she is uncertain how to express a meaning. Both F1 and F2 contribute signals which draw attention to the difficulty in communicating the meaning in English. All three interactants respond to one another's attempts to express the meaning. . . . This extended negotiation of meaning sequence demonstrates mutual or co-construction of meaning as identified by Ellis (1984) and Chaudron (1988) or what was described as cooperative building of discourse (Bygate 1987, 1988; Williams 1999). By the end of the sequence, the three learners understand the meaning (thus over-coming the communication breakdown), but they have not managed to express it in the common English phrasing: 'he died and rose again'.
>
> (Martyn 2001: 34–5)

Investigators have found that this distinction between 'simple' and 'complex' sequences is important from a research perspective. For example, Ellis, Basturkmen and Loewen (2001) found that while the majority of negotiation of meaning sequences in their data were of the simple type, the complex types resulted in significantly greater uptake on the part of subjects. In her research, Martyn (2001) also incorporated the distinction between simple and complex exchanges, but found that she needed a more sensitive measure in order to operationalize the construct of 'complex negotiation of meaning sequence'. She did this by develop-ing a technique for measuring the density of the sequences.

Density of negotiation comes in the form of three ratios: the number of signals per negotiation sequence, the number of responses per negoti-ation sequence, and the number of signals per response. A simple sequence would have one signal and one response, and therefore the ratios 1/1, 1/1 and 1/1. A sequence with two signals and five responses would have rations of 2/1, 5/1 and 2.5/1, reflecting the much greater density of the sequence. Martyn argued that calculating density rather than simple counts of instances of negotiation would provide a more accurate measure of the level of communicative demand and cognitive involvement generated by different task types.

The claim by Long and others that the negotiation of meaning is an important variable in language acquisition stimulated a substantial body of work investigating the functioning of the construct in the acquisition process. Most of these studies sought to identify the characteristics of ped-agogical tasks that stimulated negotiation of meaning. In his own work, Long found that two-way tasks, in which all students in a group had unique information to contribute, stimulated more meaning negotiation than one-way tasks, in which one student held all of the information needed to complete that task. Working in a similar tradition, Doughty and Pica (1986) found that required information exchange tasks generated significantly more negotiation than tasks in which the exchange of information was optional.

In an effort to synthesize the large number of studies in this area that had emerged by the early 1990s, Pica, Kanagy and Falodun (1993) designed a framework incorporating what they saw as the two key features of a task: the *interactional activity* and the *communication goal*. Each of these features was broken down into two subsidiary dimensions. Interactional activity consisted of *interactant relationship* and *interactant requirement*, and communication goal was broken down into *outcome options* and *goal orientation*:

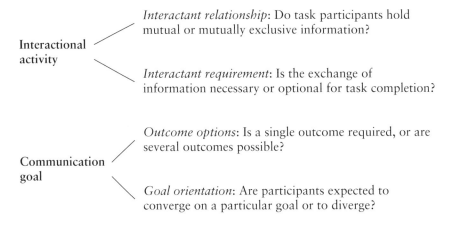

Interactional activity

Interactant relationship: Do task participants hold mutual or mutually exclusive information?

Interactant requirement: Is the exchange of information necessary or optional for task completion?

Communication goal

Outcome options: Is a single outcome required, or are several outcomes possible?

Goal orientation: Are participants expected to converge on a particular goal or to diverge?

Pica *et al.* proposed five basic task types, each of which was unique in terms of the ways in which the features combined. These were the 'jigsaw' task, the 'information exchange' task, the 'problem-solving' task, the 'decision-making' task, and the 'opinion exchange' task. They also argued that four conditions would maximize opportunities for the negotiation of meaning:

- each interactant holds a different portion of information
- it is necessary for the information to be exchanged for the task to be successfully completed
- interactants have convergent goals
- only one acceptable outcome is possible.

(Pica, Kanagy and Falodun 1993: 17)

According to Pica *et al.*'s model, a jigsaw task, which meets all four conditions, should generate the most negotiation, and an opinion exchange, which meets none, should generate the least. The other three tasks would form a continuum in between.

Task difficulty

The issue of difficulty is of central importance to researchers, curriculum developers, syllabus designers, materials writers and classroom teachers, and it is therefore not surprising that it has been the subject of considerable research. Without some way of determining difficulty, sequencing and integrating tasks becomes a matter of intuition. Sequencing linguistic exercises is somewhat more straightforward than sequencing pedagogical tasks because one can draw on notions of linguistic complexity and so on. I say 'somewhat' because work in areas such as speech processing show there are constraints other than linguistic ones that have an important effect on what is learnable at any particular stage. While research into this important area is growing, researchers have only begun to scratch the surface, and there is as yet no objective method for determining task complexity or difficulty.

When syllabus designers began experimenting with alternatives to grammatical syllabuses the issue of difficulty became more problematic. In a functional syllabus, 'apologizing' may be less difficult than 'speculating about the future', but to what extent could 'asking for directions' be seen as more or less difficult that 'making plans to meet'? Sequencing and grading language functions has remained, and will probably always remain, largely intuitive.

Determining task difficulty becomes even more problematic than determining functional difficulty. All other things being equal, what is it that makes one task more difficult than another? Brindley (1987) points out that this question is complicated by the fact that there are at least three intersecting sets of factors involved: learner factors, task factors and text or input factors. These are illustrated below:

Easier————————————————→More difficult

Learner

is confident about the task	is not confident
is motivated to carry out the task	is not motivated
has necessary prior learning experiences	has no prior experiences
can learn at pace required	cannot learn at pace required
has necessary language skills	does not have language skills
has relevant cultural knowledge	does not have relevant cultural knowledge

Easier————————————————→More difficult

Task

low cognitive complexity	cognitively complex
has few steps	has many steps
plenty of context provided	no context
plenty of help available	no help available
does not require grammatical accuracy	grammatical accuracy required
has as much time as necessary	has little time

Text / Input

is short, not dense (few facts)	is long and dense (many facts)
clear presentation	presentation not clear
plenty of contextual clues	few contextual clues
familiar, everyday content	unfamiliar content

One of the earliest series of empirical investigations into task difficulty was carried out by Brown, Anderson, Shilcock and Yule (1984). These researchers investigated the issue of what made speaking tasks difficult, and proposed a two-dimensional framework. The first dimension related to the type of information that had to be conveyed. The second dimension concerned the scale of the task and the interrelationships among the different elements involved. In relation to the first dimension, they found that 'static' tasks such as describing a diagram, in which the elements remain constant relative to each other, were easier than 'dynamic' tasks such as telling a story or describing a road accident, where the elements change relative to one another. Most difficult of all were 'abstract' tasks such as expressing an opinion, in which the elements are abstract rather than concrete.

> **Reflect**
> In your experience, which of the factors discussed in this section contribute most to task difficulty? Which factors are intentional and can be manipulated to make tasks more or less challenging, and which are beyond the teacher's control (e.g. 'learner background knowledge')?

Of all these factors, it is probably 'cognitive complexity / demand' that has attracted most attention from researchers. Two researchers who have most clearly articulated and researched the concept of cognitive complexity are Skehan (1998) and Robinson (2001a). Skehan, drawing on earlier work by Candlin (1987), set out to develop a scheme that would make complexity criteria and actual tasks transparent. His model proposes a three-way distinction between code complexity (this relates to the language required), cognitive complexity (the thinking required), and communicative stress (the performance conditions demanded by the task). These are elaborated as follows:

Code complexity   linguistic complexity and variety, vocabulary load and variety, redundancy and density.

Cognitive complexity
   Cognitive familiarity: familiarity of topic and its predictability, familiarity of discourse genre, familiarity of task.
   Cognitive processing: information organization, amount of 'computation', clarity and sufficient information given, information type.

Communicative stress   time limits and time pressure, speed of presentation, number of participants, length of texts used, type of response, opportunities to control interaction.

The distinction drawn by Skehan between cognitive familiarity and cognitive processing is an interesting one. Cognitive familiarity refers to the ability of the learner to access 'packaged' solutions to tasks, whereas cognitive processing refers to the need to work out solutions 'on line'.

> For example, one might compare the family tree task (comparing one another's family tree in pairs) and a riddle task (both taken from Willis and Willis (1988). In the former case, the task requires existing well-organized 'chunks' of knowledge to be retrieved and mobilized for task performance. In the latter, elements of a task are easy to handle, but there is significant difficulty in manipulating them to achieve a solution that the task requires. It is assumed that in the former case attentional resources are not particularly stretched, and there is scope for a focus on form (VanPatten 1994). In the latter, where processing has to be directed at the cognitive problem involved, there is less attention left over to focus on form.
> (Skehan 1998: 100)

The other aspect of Skehan's work that is particularly interesting is his system for measuring task complexity in performance (see also Foster and Skehan 1996, 1997). The model developed by Foster and Skehan incorporates three dimensions of task performance: accuracy, complexity and fluency. Accuracy is measured by dividing the number of correct clauses by the total number of clauses produced by each subject. Complexity is measured by dividing the total number of clauses by the total number of C-units produced by each subject. (A C-unit is an utterance containing a unit of referential or pragmatic meaning.) Fluency is measured by the total number of seconds of silence and time spent saying 'um' and 'ah' by subjects as they complete a task.

Foster and Skehan found that different kinds of tasks made different types of cognitive demand. In their study, they used three different kinds of tasks, which they labelled as 'personal', 'narration', and decision-making'. The personal information exchange task required one subject to tell another how to get to their home to turn off a gas oven that they had left on. In the narrative task, subjects had to construct a story based on a sequence of pictures. In the decision-making task, subjects had to role play a judge and decide on appropriate punishments for wrong-doers. 'The three tasks essentially opposed familiar with unfamiliar propositions, and clear structure for the information required with progressively less predictable structure and interaction' (Skehan 1998: 108). Foster and Skehan found that accuracy was significantly higher on the personal and decision-making tasks than on the narrative. The personal task generated less complex language than the narrative and the decision-making task. Finally, subjects displayed significantly less fluency on the narrative and decision-making tasks compared with the personal task.

Robinson (2001b) also found that cognitive complexity was anything but a unitary construct. In his model, he argues that cognitive factors are either resource-directing or resource-depleting. Resource-directing factors include the number of elements involved, the amount of contextual support available, and the reasoning demands made on the user. Resource-depleting factors, so called because they make demands on attention and working memory, include the amount of planning time available, whether the task makes single or dual demands and the extent to which the learner has relevant prior knowledge. Any of the factors can be manipulated to increase or decrease the complexity of a task in terms of its cognitive demand.

Robinson links his cognitive demand framework to the negotiation of meaning by arguing that . . .

> . . . complex versions of tasks should result in more negotiation, and consequently more confirmation checks and clarification requests than simpler versions. . . . More interaction and turn-taking may mitigate speakers' attempts to produce complex syntax and subordination, resulting in greater numbers of elliptical yes/no or single clause answers to clarification requests and confirmation checks relative to performance on less interactively negotiated simple versions of a task.
>
> (Robinson 2001b: 36)

For her research, Martyn (2001) isolated from the literature four key conditions of cognitive demand. There were:

Contextual support: whether embedded, reduced or remote
Reasoning demand: whether high or low
Degree of task structure: whether high or low

Availability of knowledge schema: provided or assumed through prior knowledge.

She then mapped these onto the five-task framework adapted from Pica *et al.* as follows:

Task type	Cognitive demand features			
	Contextual support	Reasoning required	Degree of task structure	Available knowledge
Jigsaw	embedded	not required	high	given
Information exchange	embedded (for one learner)	not required	high	given
Problem-solving	some embedded	required	varies	given
Decision-making	context-reduced	required	low	given or available
Opinion exchange	remote	required	low	variable/not required

(Adapted from Martyn 2001)

Drawing on density of negotiation, the construct she developed for meas-uring the level of communicative demand and cognitive involvement generated by different task types, she hypothesized that the five tasks would range on a continuum according to the density of negotiation sequences generated by each, that the jigsaw would produce the lowest density of negotiation of meaning, and the opinion exchange would produce the highest, with the remaining tasks on a continuum in between. The jigsaw makes the least cognitive demand because the context is embedded in the task information and it must be shared, no reasoning is required, it is highly structured by the number and type of items to be exchanged, and the knowledge schema is provided by the task. In the opinion exchange, on the other hand, the context is remote as a result of the abstract nature of the task, reasoning is required in the presentation of opinions, there is a low level of structure as there is no required information exchange and agreement on a single outcome is not required, the goals are divergent, and the knowledge schema need not be provided as the outcome is open.

Martyn's incorporation of cognitive demand into research on negoti-ation of meaning is significant. Previous researchers had argued that, based on frequency counts of instances of negotiation, jigsaw tasks would generate the most, and opinion exchange tasks the least negotiation. However, Martyn argued that when density of negotiation was the dependent variable the result would be reversed, that the opinion exchange task, having greater cognitive demand, would generate negotiation of meaning sequences with significantly higher density. Her research generally supported this hypothesis. She found that jigsaw and information exchange tasks generated a lower density of negotiation of meaning sequences than the problem-solving, decision-making and opinion-exchange tasks.

This research outcome has important theoretical and practical implications. Tasks with high cognitive demand and more complex communication, as marked by high density negotiation of meaning sequences, generate the 'pushed output' that Swain (1995) argued was a factor in second language acquisition. With learners at an appropriate level of proficiency, they could therefore facilitate acquisition. On the other hand, if the learners are not at an appropriate level of proficiency, the tasks could, as Skehan (1993) suggests, lead to an overload of their processing capacity which in turn could lead to fossilization rather than acquisition.

Conclusion

In recent years, there has been an explosion in the number of investigations into various aspects of task-based learning and teaching. Far too many studies have been conducted to be covered in detail in this chapter. For this reason, I have elected to provide a selective coverage of those studies that have been most influential in setting directions for both research and practice.

In the first part of the chapter, I reviewed some of the early psycholinguistically motivated studies that provided a rationale for Krashen's hypotheses. While these hypotheses have proved controversial, and have been subjected to a great deal of criticism, they remain popular today, and continue to attract a great deal of interest.

The 'second wave' of research set off by the work of Krashen and others embraced 'interaction', 'output' and the 'negotiation of meaning' as key constructs, and looked for relationships between these constructs and second language acquisition. This research posits an indirect relationship between the negotiation of meaning and second language acquisition.

In the final part of the chapter, I covered some of the research into task difficulty and complexity. This review led us into the area of cognition, and the construct of cognitive complexity. Here, I revisited the concept of negotiation of meaning and suggested that *density* of negotiation is an important element in our search for relationships between task types, cognitive complexity and second language acquisition.

References

Bailey, K. 1999. What have we learned from 25 years of classroom research? Plenary presentation, International TESOL Convention, New York, March 1999.

Brindley, G. 1987. Factors affecting task difficulty. In D. Nunan (ed.) *Guidelines for the Development of Curriculum Resources*. Adelaide: National Curriculum Resource Centre.

Brown, G., A. Anderson, R. Shilcock and G. Yule. 1984. *Teaching Talk: Strategies for production and assessment*. Cambridge: Cambridge University Press.

Bygate, M. 1987. *Speaking*. Oxford: Oxford University Press.

Bygate, M. 1988. Units of oral expression and language learning in small group interaction. *Applied Linguistics*, 9, 69–82.

Candlin, C. 1987. Toward task-based learning. In C. Candlin and D. Murphy (eds) *Language Learning Tasks*. Englewood Cliffs NJ: Prentice Hall.

Chaudron, C. 1988. *Second Language Classrooms: Research on teaching and learning*. Cambridge: Cambridge University Press.

Doughty, C. and T. Pica. 1986. 'Information gap' tasks: Do they facilitate second language acquisition? *TESOL Quarterly*, 20, 2.

Dulay, H. and M. Burt. 1973. Should we teach children syntax? *Language Learning*, 23.

Dulay, H. and M. Burt. 1974. Natural sequences in child second language acquisition. *Language Learning*, 24.

Ellis, R. 1984. *Classroom Second Language Development: a study of classroom interaction and language acquisition*. Oxford: Pergamon Press.

Ellis, R., H. Basturmen and S. Loewen. 2001. Learner uptake in communicative ESL lessons. *Language Learning*, 51, 281–318.

Foster, P. and P. Skehan. 1996. The influence of planning on performance in task-based learning. *Studies in Second Language Acquisition*, 18, 299–324.

Foster, P. and P. Skehan. 1997. Modifying the task: the effects of surprise, time and planning type on task-based foreign language instruction. *Thames Valley University Working Papers in English Language Teaching*. Volume 4.

Hatch, E. 1978. Discourse analysis and second language acquisition. In E. Hatch (ed.) *Second Language Acquisition: a book of readings*. Rowley Mass.: Newbury House.

Krashen, S. 1981. *Second Language Acquisition and Second Language Learning*. Oxford: Pergamon Press.

Krashen, S. 1982. *Principles and Practice in Second Language Acquisition*. Oxford: Pergamon Press.

Long, M. 1985. Input and second language acquisition theory. In S. Gass and C. Madden (eds) *Input in Second Language Acquisition*. Rowley Mass.: Newbury House.

Martyn, E. 2001. The effect of task type on negotiation of meaning in small group work. Unpublished doctoral dissertation, University of Hong Kong.

Nunan, D. 2005. Classroom-based research. In E. Hinkel (ed.) *Handbook of Research in Second Language Teaching and Learning*. Mahwah, NJ: Lawrence Erlbaum.

Pica, T., L. Holliday, N. Lewis, D. Berducci and J. Newman. 1991. Second language learning through interaction: What role does gender play? *Studies in Second Language Acquisition*, 11, 152–187.

Pica, T., R. Kanagy and J. Falodun. 1993. Choosing and using communication tasks for second language instruction and research. In G. Crookes and S. Gass (eds) *Tasks and Language Learning: Integrating theory and practice*. Clevedon, Avon: Multilingual Matters.

Robinson, P. 2001a. *Cognition and Second Language Instruction*. Cambridge: Cambridge University Press.

Robinson, P. 2001b. Task complexity, task difficulty, and task production: Exploring interactions in a componential framework. *Applied Linguistics*, 22, 27–57.

Shehadeh, A. 1999. Non-native speakers' production of modified comprehensible output and second language learning. *Language Learning*, 49, 627–75.

Skehan, P. 1993. Second language acquisition and task-based learning. In M. Bygate and E. Williams (eds) *Grammar in the L2 Classroom*. New York: Prentice-Hall.

Skehan, P. 1998. *A Cognitive Approach to Language Learning*. Oxford: Oxford University Press.

Swain, M. 1985. Communicative competence: Some roles for comprehensible input and comprehensible output in its development. In S. Gass and C. Madden (eds) *Input in Second Language Acquisition*. Rowley Mass.: Newbury House.

Swain, M. 1995. Three functions of output in second language learning. In G. Cook and B. Seidlhofer (eds) *Principles and Practice in Applied Linguistics: Studies in honour of H. G. Widdowson*. Oxford: Oxford University Press.

VanPatten, B. 1994. Evaluating the role of consciousness in SLA: Terms, linguistic features, and research methodology. *AILA Review*, 11, 27–36.

Williams, J. 1999. Learner-generated attention to form. *Language Learning*, 49, 583–625.

Willis, D. and J. Willis. 1988. *COBUILD Book 1*. London: Collins.

5 Focus on form in task-based language teaching

Introduction and overview

The purpose of this chapter is to take a more detailed look at the place of grammar instruction within task-based language teaching. As we have already seen, the issue of whether or not a focus on form has a place in task-based language teaching is controversial. In the first section of the chapter, I will review several theoretical and empirical aspects of form-focused instruction that are of significance to TBLT. I will then expand on two of these: form-focused versus unfocused tasks, and consciousness-raising tasks. The sections that follow then focuses on an issue of central importance to syllabus designers and materials writers, which is where form-focused work should come in any task-based instructional cycle.

Theoretical and empirical issues

As we saw in Chapter 4, the place of a focus on form in TBLT is controversial. Some theorists adopt a 'strong' interpretation, arguing that communicative interaction in the language is necessary and sufficient for language acquisition, and that a focus on form is unnecessary. Krashen (1981, 1982), whose work was examined in detail in the preceding chapter, is one of the main proponents of this 'strong' approach. He argues that there are two processes operating in language development, subconscious acquisition and conscious learning, and that form-focused instruction is aimed at conscious learning which does not feed in to subconscious acquisition.

Another major issue for TBLT concerns the relationship between the task and the language that supports it or through which it is realized. Here the question is whether a particular grammatical structure is required in order for a task to be completed successfully, or whether it is possible to complete a task successfully using whatever linguistic tasks are at one's disposal. Proponents of a 'strong' interpretation of TBLT believe very firmly in the latter view, that learners should be able to use whatever linguistic means they can muster, and that an approach which imposes linguistic constraints can not be called 'task-based'. As this is such an important issue I will look at it in detail in the next section.

A relatively new approach to the study of language acquisition in instructional contexts is 'sociocultural theory' (Lantolf 2000). This approach has challenged the prevailing psycholinguistic tradition, which has dominated research into the place of a focus on form in the language classroom. It is based on the theories of the Russian psychologist Vygotsky, who viewed language as a social as well as a cognitive tool through which humans are able to act upon and change the world in which they live. Researchers using this approach study the interactions between two or more language learners as they complete a task to see how their collaborative interactions provide opportunities for second language learning. This typically occurs when one of the participants has a piece of linguistic knowledge that the other doesn't, or when the learners collaboratively co-construct a piece of knowledge inductively. The ultimate aim of researchers working in this area is to demonstrate how collaborative conversations provide opportunities for second language learning.

Focused versus unfocused tasks

A key issue for TBLT is whether the tasks themselves should be focused or unfocused. A focused task is one in which a particular structure is required in order for a task to be completed. An unfocused task is one in which the learners are able to use any linguistic resources at their disposal in order to complete the task.

Consider the following discussion task that occurs in a unit of work on the topic of 'Inventions':

⋙▸

What are the five most helpful inventions and the five most annoying inventions? Make a list. Then explain your opinion.

Helpful inventions	Annoying inventions
Example: *telephone*	Example: *alarm clock*
1.	1.
2.	2.
3.	3.
4.	4.
5.	5.

(Nunan 2000: 63)

It might reasonably be predicted that learners would need to use super-latives ('most helpful', 'most annoying'), as well as clauses of reason 'because', coming up with statements such as, 'I think the most helpful invention is the light bulb, because they give people more time to work and play every day.' However, there are numerous other ways in which the task might be completed without the use of these particular forms, such as: 'I hate alarm clocks. They drive me nuts. I go to bed late and I like to sleep in.' In fact, the number of tasks in which it is possible to predict, with a high degree of certainty, the exact grammatical structures the learners will use is probably relatively small.

In discussing the issue of whether a task can or should predetermine a particular grammatical form, Loschky and Bley-Vroman (1993) make a number of useful comments. They point out that, while a particular form may not be essential for the successful completion of a task, certain forms (such as the ones in the task above) could be expected to arise quite naturally in the course of the task. They also point out, that while linguistic

Focus on form in task-based language teaching

forms targeted by the curriculum, the textbook or the teacher might not be essential, the use of such forms will greatly facilitate the completion of the task. They cite spot-the-difference tasks such as the following.

 Student 1 looks at the picture on this page, and Student 2 looks at the picture on page 96. Ask and answer questions to find the differences between the pictures. Use the questions in the box.

| Does Joe have a...? | Where is the...? | | Is the... in/on/under the...? |
| Does his sister/mother/father have a...? | | Is there a...? | What color is...? |

Student 2

(Nunan 2003: 65 and 96)

This task is designed to elicit the use of prepositions (among other forms). Loschky and Bley-Vroman (1993) point out that, while the task can be completed without the use of prepositions, using prepositions will make the task easier to complete, and could well facilitate a more successful outcome than if prepositions were not used by the learners taking part in the task.

Willis and Willis (2001: 173–4) reject the notion of 'focused' (or, as they call them, 'metacommunicative') tasks:

> The use of the word 'task' is sometimes extended to include 'metacommunicative tasks', or exercises with a focus on linguistic form, in which learners manipulate language or formulate generalizations about form. But a definition of task which includes an explicit focus on form seems to be so all-embracing as to cover almost anything that might happen in a classroom. We therefore restrict our use of the term 'task' to communicative tasks and exclude metacommunicative tasks from our definition. One feature of TBL (task-based learning), therefore, is that learners carrying out a task are free to use any language they can to achieve the outcomes: language forms are not prescribed in advance.

However, this does not mean that an instructional sequence should not include a form-focused exercise – merely that it should not be called a 'task'.

Reflect

Study the following procedure. Is it focused or unfocused? If it is focused, what is the focus and how is this focus achieved? Would you say that it is a pedagogical task, a communicative activity or a language exercise?

11.3 Detectives

Procedure: An object to be 'stolen' is decided on – say a coin or a ring. One student (the 'detective') is sent out of the room. One of the remaining students is given the object; he or she is the 'thief'. The detective returns and tries to find out who the thief is by asking participants:

Do you have it / the ring?

Each participant – including the actual thief – denies guilt, and accuses someone else:

No, I don't have it. A has it!

⋙→

> Whereupon, the detective turns to A with the same question – and so on, until everyone has been asked and has denied responsibility. The detective then has to decide in three guesses who is lying – who 'looks guilty'. The process is then repeated with another detective and another thief.
>
> Variations: The activity may be made more lively by encouraging students to act innocence or indignation as convincingly as they can: they may change the emphasis or intonation of the set sentences as they wish, add gestures and so on. Another technique, which abandons verisimilitude but helps fluency, is to get the class to complete the round of 'interrogations' as quickly as possible ('Let's see if we can get round the whole class in two minutes' . . . 'Let's see if we can do it again in even less time').

(Ur, P. 1988: 123–4)

Consciousness-raising tasks

Ellis (2001) argues for a particular variant of focused tasks that he calls consciousness-raising (CR) tasks. Consciousness-raising tasks are designed to draw learners' attention to a particular linguistic feature through a range of inductive and deductive procedures. The assumption here is not that a feature once raised to consciousness will be immediately incorporated into the learner's interlanguage, but that it is a first step in that direction.

Ellis states that consciousness-raising tasks differ from other focused tasks in two essential ways:

> First, whereas structure-based production tasks, enriched input tasks and interpretation tasks are intended to cater primarily to implicit learning, CR-tasks are designed to cater primarily to explicit learning – that is, they are intended to develop awareness at the level of 'understanding' rather than awareness at the level of 'noticing' (see Schmidt 1994). Thus, the desired outcome of a CR-task is awareness of how some linguistic feature works. Second, whereas the previous types of task were built around content of a general nature (e.g. stories, pictures of objects, opinions about the kind of person you like), CR-tasks make language itself the content. In this respect, it can be asked whether CR-tasks are indeed tasks. They are in the sense that learners are required to talk meaningfully about a language point using their own linguistic resources. That is, although there is some linguistic feature that is the focus of the task learners are not required to use this feature, only think about it and discuss it. The 'taskness' of a CR-task lies

98

not in the linguistic point that is the focus of the task but rather in the talk learners must engage in in order to achieve an outcome to the task.

(Ellis 2001: 162–3)

In designing CR tasks, the first step is to isolate a specific feature for attention. The learners are provided with input data illustrating the feature, and may also be given a rule to explain the feature. They are then required either to understand it, or (if they have not been given the rule) to describe the grammatical structure in question.

The following example of a CR task is provided by Fotos and Ellis (1991).

A. What is the difference between verbs like 'give' and 'explain'?

She gave a book to her father (= grammatical)
She gave her father a book (= grammatical)

The policeman explained the law to Mary (= grammatical)
The policeman explained Mary the law (= ungrammatical).

B. Indicate whether the following sentences are grammatical or ungrammatical.

1. They saved Mark a seat.
2. His father read Kim a story.
3. She donated the hospital some money.
4. They suggested Mary a trip on the river.
5. They reported the police the accident.
6. They threw Mary a party.
7. The bank lent Mr Thatcher some money.
8. He indicated Mary the right turning.
9. The festival generated the college a lot of money.
10. He cooked his girlfriend a cake.

C. Work out a rule for verbs like 'give' and 'explain'.

1. List the verbs in B that are like 'give' (i.e. permit both sentence patterns) and those that are like 'explain' (i.e. allow only one sentence pattern).
2. What is the difference between the verbs in your two lists?[3]

---

3 This example from Ellis is interesting because it does not appear in any standard grammar reference books. Despite this, advanced learners of English are able to identify several 'rules' or principles (Ellis, personal communication). One of these is that the verbs permitting both patterns are from Old English, whereas the others are from Greek or Latin. The number of syllables is also a factor.

Procedural language

In addition to the language forms inherent in a given task, there is also the procedural language that is generated by two or more individuals in the course of completing a task. This procedural language, which is a kind of 'byproduct' of the task, will include conversational management language such as:

bidding for a turn
agreeing and disagreeing
negotiating meaning
hesitating and hedging.

Reflect
Consider the following decision-making task. Is this a focused or unfocused task? What procedural and content language do you think might be needed in order to complete the task? What grammatical knowledge might be needed? If possible, get a group of upper-intermediate or advanced learners to complete the task. Record and analyze their language. Were your predictions confirmed?

Sahara Survival

It is approximately 10.00 am in mid-July and you have just crashed in the Sahara Desert. The light twin-engine plane, containing the bodies of the pilot and co-pilot, has completely burnt out. Only the frame remains. None of the rest of you has been injured.

The pilot was unable to notify anyone of your position before the crash. However, ground sightings, taken before you crashed, indicated that you were 65 miles off the course that was filed in your flight plan. The pilot indicated before you crashed that you were approximately 70 miles south-south-west from a small oasis, which is the nearest known habitation.

The immediate area is quite flat and, except for occasional cacti, seems to be rather barren. The last weather report indicated that the temperature will reach 110 degrees F, which means that the temperature within a foot of the surface will reach 130 degrees F. You are dressed in lightweight clothes – short-sleeved shirts, shorts or skirts, socks and shoes or sandals. Everyone has a handkerchief.

Before the plane caught fire, your group was able to salvage the 15 items listed below. Your task is to rank the items according to the importance for your survival starting with 1 (the most important) and finishing with 15 (the least important).

The items

- Flashlight
- Pen knife
- Map of the area
- Plastic raincoat
- Magnetic compass
- First-aid kit
- Pistol (loaded)
- Parachute
- Bottle of salt tablets
- 1 quart of water per person
- A pair of sunglasses per person
- 5 bottles of vodka
- 1 coat per person
- A cosmetic mirror
- A book entitled *Edible Animals of the Desert*

(Adapted from an EDEXEL A-level Psychology simulation)

The place of a focus on form in an instructional sequence

For those who accept the value in having a focus on form at some point in the instructional cycle, there is an ongoing question as to where such a focus should come in the cycle. In early versions of task-based language teaching, the tendency was to introduce the focus on form first, at what was called the 'pre-communicative stage' of a lesson or unit of work. This was intended to provide a basis for later communicative work, the argument being that it was unrealistic to expect learners to be able to use language that they had not been explicitly taught. In practice, this approach was very little different from the 3Ps (presentation, practice, production) instructional cycle that it was designed to replace.

In Chapter 2, I presented a six-step pedagogical sequence which shows where I believe that a focus on form should come, that is, at step 4 in the sequence. There are several reasons for placing it here, rather than at the beginning of the sequence. Firstly, the sequence begins with a focus on the communicative ends rather than the linguistic means. In the steps prior to this, learners get to see, hear and use the target language from a communicative or pseudo-communicative perspective. They get to see and hear the language being used communicatively by native speakers or competent second language speakers. Hopefully, this will make it easier for the learners to establish links between the linguistic forms and the communicative functions they realise.

> **Reflect**
> Consider the following task and exercise types from the
> *Interchange* series. Which types provide an opportunity for a focus
> on form? How would you sequence these types into an instruc-
> tional sequence? What is the rationale for your sequencing?

Task/exercise type	Description
Snapshot	The snapshots graphically present interesting real-world information that introduces the topic of a unit or cycle, and also develop vocabulary. Follow-up questions encourage discussion of the snapshot material and personalize the topic.
Conversation	The conversations introduce the new grammar of each cycle in a communicative context and present functional and conversational expressions.
Grammar focus	The new grammar of each unit is presented in color boxes and is followed by controlled and freer communicative practice activities. These freer activities often have students use the grammar in a personal context.
Fluency exercise	These pair, group, whole class, or role-play activities provide more personal practice of the new teaching points and increase the opportunity for individual student practice.
Pronunciation	These exercises focus on important features of spoken English, including stress, rhythm, intonation, reductions and blending.
Listening	The listening activities develop a wide variety of listening skills, including listening for gist, listening for details, and inferring meaning from context. Charts or graphics often accompany these task-based exercises to lend support to students.
Word power	The word power activities develop students' vocabulary through a variety of interesting tasks, such as word maps and collocation exercises. Word power activities are usually followed by oral and written practice that helps students understand how to use the vocabulary in context.

⟫➤

Writing	The writing exercises include practical writing tasks that extend and reinforce the teaching points in the unit and help develop students' compositional skills. The Teacher's Edition demonstrates how to use the models and exercises to focus on the process of writing.
Reading	The reading passages use various types of texts adapted from authentic sources. The readings develop a variety of reading skills, including reading for details, skimming, scanning and making inferences. Also included are pre-reading and post-reading questions that use the topic of the reading as a spring board to discussion.
Interchange activities	The interchange activities are pair work, group work, or whole class activities involving information sharing and role playing to encourage real communication. These exercises are a central part of the course and allow students to extend and personalize what they have practised and learned in each unit.

(Adapted from Richards, Hull and Proctor 1997: iv – v)

A unit based on this task/exercise typology is reproduced as Appendix C.

> **Reflect**
> Compare the two units of work presented as Appendices B and C.
> What similarities and differences do you notice between the two
> units? (Look, for example, at the sequencing of tasks and exercises.
> Do listening and speaking tasks come before reading and writing?
> When is a focus on grammar introduced? How is it introduced?
> What are learners expected to do?)

Focus on form in the communicative classroom

In this section, I would like to demonstrate some of the ways in which a focus on form can be integrated into task work in the classroom. In the lesson extract that follows, the students are completing an information gap task. The pedagogical objectives are asking about and making suggestions using Wh-questions with 'do' and 'like' 'like +Ving'. The task illustrates principle 2 – use tasks that show the relationship between form and function. Unlike the other teaching sequences in this section,

Focus on form in task-based language teaching

the grammar is presented within a context that makes clear to the learners one communicative use for the structure. It also illustrates the way that both declarative knowledge and procedural knowledge can be worked in to a pedagogical sequence.

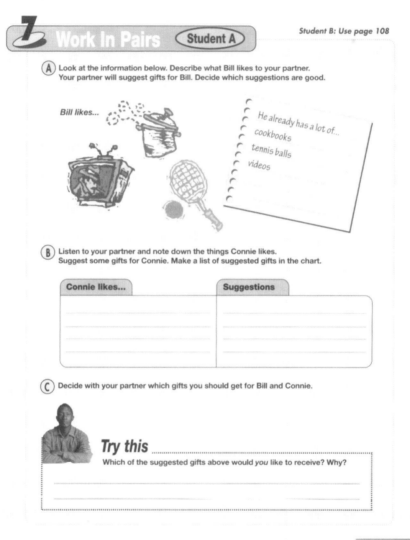

104

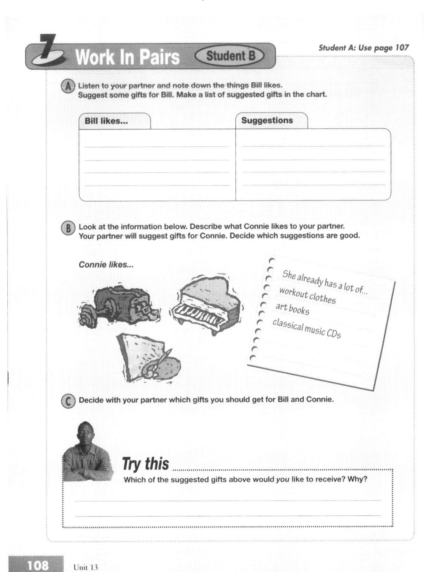

Work In Pairs — Student B

Student A: Use page 107

A Listen to your partner and note down the things Bill likes.
Suggest some gifts for Bill. Make a list of suggested gifts in the chart.

Bill likes...	Suggestions

B Look at the information below. Describe what Connie likes to your partner.
Your partner will suggest gifts for Connie. Decide which suggestions are good.

Connie likes...

She already has a lot of...
workout clothes
art books
classical music CDs

C Decide with your partner which gifts you should get for Bill and Connie.

Try this

Which of the suggested gifts above would *you* like to receive? Why?

108 Unit 13

(Nunan 2001: 107–8)

T: Right, now are you ready to do the info gap task? Yes? We've done lots of these, now, haven't we?

Ss: (nod)

T: The purpose of this task is to give you more practice in the language we're learning in this unit. What ARE we practising? Remember? Johnny?

S: Talk about what people like.

T: Talking about what people like – good. And?

S: Talking about gift giving.

T: Talking about gift giving. Right. These are our communication goals. And what structures do we use to do these things? . . . Anyone? . . . Yes, Mary?

S: *What do you like?* And *What do you like doing?*

T: Great! And we use *like* to talk about things, right? And *like doing* to talk about activities. What about making gift-giving suggestions?

S: *Let's.*

T: OK, good, *Let's get him a CD*, or *Let's get Tom a golf club*. OK, now WHEN do we give people gifts? WHEN? Yes, Monica?

S: Birthday.

T: Birthdays are good. (Writes *birthdays* on the board.) Johnny?

S: New . . . new baby.

T: That's a good suggestion. (Writes *new baby* on the board and continues eliciting until there are a number of events on the board.) OK, now get into your pairs and I want Student A to look at page 107, and Student B to look at page 108. . . . (Peers over students' shoulder) Johnny, you're the B student, aren't you? You're looking at the wrong page. 108, please. Good. Now, Bill likes the things the A students can see in the picture, but he already has these things. OK? Understand, Monica? Right. So, tell your partner what Bill likes, and your partner will suggest gifts. Write the suggestion in the space, and then decide on the best idea. OK, Student A – start off by suggesting a reason for buying a gift – look at the board – it's his birthday, he's going away and so on. Right, off you go.

(The students complete the task. As they do so, the teacher circulates and monitors. When she hears a mistake, she writes it in a notebook, but doesn't interrupt the students.)

OK, I think everybody's finished now. Are you two finished? Right, good. So, now I want you to do the same thing for Connie. B, tell A what Connie likes. A will make suggestions. Write them down then decide, decide on the best one, OK?

(Again, the teacher circulates and monitors. At one point she is stopped by one pair, listens to their question and says 'It's called a sub-scription – a subscription'.)

> OK, time's up. Let's hear what each pair decided. (Teacher elicits responses from the students and writes them on the board.) Well, that's great – look at all these interesting gifts. Which of these gifts would YOU like to receive, Johnny? . . . Sorry?
> S: The California Fitness Subscription.
> T: Yeah, I like that one too. How about you, Sophie? (She continues, eliciting students' preferences, and writing their names next to the gift.) OK, Now, you all did very well, but I noticed a few mistakes creeping in here and there. Look. (She writes the mistakes from her notebook on the board, and gets students to self-correct.)

I like this piece of classroom interaction for a number of reasons. In the first place, it demonstrates an effective teacher in action. At the beginning of the sequence, the teacher sets out the pedagogical agenda for the students. While the overall focus of the sequence is on the communicative task, she skilfully links the communicative goal of the lesson with the grammatical exponents that will help the students as they complete the task. In addition, she demonstrates excellent elicitation skills, drawing information from the students rather than simply telling them. As the students complete the task, she actively monitors them, providing models when necessary, and helps one pair out when they encounter a difficulty. In the post-task debriefing, she personalizes the task, and provides form-focused feedback on errors she noted as the students completed the task.

Samuda (2001) suggests that in setting up a task the teacher can provide either an implicit or an explicit focus on target language structures. She exemplifies these two teaching strategies in relation to a task designed to elicit the expressions of probability and possibility. Students working in small groups were provided with a set of objects that were supposedly the contents of a person's pocket. They had to speculate on the identity of the person, come to a conclusion and justify that conclusion. In doing the task, each group had to fill in the following chart, registering the degree of probability / possibility in relation to each conclusion.

How certain are you?			
	Less than 50% certain (It's possible)	90% certain (It's probable)	100% certain. (It's certain)
Name			
Sex			
Age			
Marital status			
Occupation			
Habits			

Reflect
What role is the teacher playing in each of the following extracts?

Extract 1

S1: Habits?
Y: Well, first he smokes.
C: But we think uh 50% we think just 50%.
N: Yes, just maybe. We're not sure.
T: Oh yeah? Only <u>50%</u>? Why's that?
S2: Yes, give proof.
N: Because here (showing matchbox). A matchbox.
T: Hmm, but you're <u>not certain</u> if he smokes, huh? (looking at match box).
A: Look (opens matchbox). Many matches, so maybe he just keep for friend, not for him (laughter).
T: Hmm, I guess <u>it's possible</u> he might smoke. It's hard to tell just from this.
A: Yeah, not sure.
S2: You have more proof?

(Samuda 2001: 129)

Here, the teacher is playing the role of group participant. In the course of the interaction, she also provides models of the target language. However, she does not draw attention to the language; rather it remains implicit.

Extract 2

T: So, lots of interesting ideas here. Paula, letters, schedule, opera, a busy man.
C: Japanese classes.
T: Yeah, right, I forgot he's learning Japanese too (laughter).
N: And golf.
T: Oh, yes, very busy (laughter). Hmmm, let's – why don't we look at how the language works here? Just for a minute uhh (looking at objects). Let's see now. Did you have anything here that you thought was probable? Like 90%?
Y: Businessman.
T: Businessman? 90%. OK, so you're 90% certain he's a businessman, right? Here's another way to say this. You think it's 90% certain, so you think he must be a businessman. He must be a businessman (writes it on board). So this (points to must be on board) is showing how CERTAIN how SURE you are. Not 100%, but almost 100%. 90%.
A: So 100% is 'be' or 'must'?
T: 100? 100%? Then you can say he IS a businessman (writes on board) When you when you're NOT 100% certain you can use must OK? No he is a businessman but he must be a businessman. So 'be' here (pointing to 'must be' on board) is from this verb (pointing to is). Let's uh what other things do you have for probably?
C: Travel a lot.
T: OK, so if it's 90% you can say he must travel a lot (writes on board). So we use uh we use must with the verb (pointing).

(Samuda 2001: 131)

In this second extract, the teacher adopts a much more overtly instructional role, focusing students explicitly on the form–meaning relationships in question. It may well be that it is this explicit focus which leads A to seek clarification ('So 100% is "be" or "must"?') two-thirds of the way through the extract.

Samuda's study highlights the complementary relationship between the task and the teacher:

> . . . an important role for the *task* may be to attract initial attention to designated areas of meaning, and through task operations create a need to mean; an important role for the *teacher* may be to complement the task by guiding attention towards form-meaning relationships. In particular, it has suggested that task input data may play a significant, although hitherto overlooked, role as a resource to be 'mined' by learners and teachers in different ways and for different purposes during task performance.
>
> (Samuda 2001: 137)

> **Reflect**
> Explore the place of grammar in a language lesson by trying out
> the following observation task from Wajnryb 1992: 85–7.

Before the lesson

Arrange to observe a lesson in which grammar will have some place. If
possible, speak to the teacher in advance of the lesson, and discuss the
lesson's aims in terms of its grammatical focus.

During the lesson

Keep an ethnographic record of the lesson. This means that you note
down chronologically the main events in the lesson and their impact.
This will have to be brief and synoptic enough for you to keep records
'in real time'. It does not have to include scripted actual language but
rather a report of what was said and done. For example:

T enters . . . greets whole class from the front of room. T announces
what the lesson is going to be about today. T reminds SS how this lesson
follows on from yesterday's. . . . T drills new pattern . . . S asks question
about the form of the verb in pattern on board . . . T explains. S seems
to be satisfied but another S continues to ask similar questions.

After the lesson

For the purposes of the following questions, you should bear in mind
your memory of the lesson and the specific contexts in which the events
occurred as well as your written narrative record of the lesson.

1. To what extent was an aspect of grammar the central focus of the
   lesson you observed?
2. Were the students consciously involved in thinking about grammar?
   Was a rule or rules presented to them or were they expected to work
   the rules out for themselves? Were they helped or taught how to do
   this?
3. Describe the lesson in terms of 'knowing' or 'doing': Were the students finding out how the language works or were they doing something with the language? Or both? And to what degrees?
4. If the students were at any time involved in doing something with
   the language, to what extent did the tasks or activities require them
   to make connections or inferences about the system of language?
5. Was there any evidence of a range of learning styles among the
   students in terms of how they reacted to a lesson involving

grammar? Did these learning styles contrast with the teaching style in any way?

6. Have you any comments on the language used by the teacher to talk about language and how this facilitated access to understanding the language?

7. Consider now any discussion about language that took place in the classroom, either among students, or involving the teacher. From the discussion, was there any evidence of learners trying to align new information with old – that is, processing recent input with their existing hypotheses about language?

8. Is it possible to summarise:
   - what the students might have thought the lesson's objective was?
   - what they came away with from the lesson?

   Now contrast the lesson's objectives and its process.

   Do you consider that it is important that students know what the lesson is going to be about and what objectives are set? Is it important that they come away from the lesson with what the teacher plans for them to come away with?

9. Considering the lesson you observed and the discussions you have had, what inferences can you draw from the lesson about (a) what language is, and (b) what language learning is to the teacher concerned? In other words, what theories (perhaps subconscious) underline the teacher's methodology? You may wish to pursue this in a discussion with the teacher.

10. In the debate about the place of grammar in teaching, one attempt to classify teaching according to the role of grammar is that proposed by Gibbons (1989) in his description of *focused* versus *unfocused instructional cycles*. Focused instructional cycles have a particular language item focus, such as a point of grammar, whereas unfocused instructional cycles are more likely to be skills or activity based. You may wish to map this lesson that you have observed onto Gibbons's schemata in order to deepen your understanding of how grammar features.

Conclusion

In this chapter, I have explored the place of a focus on form in TBLT. As indeed, in the rest of the book, I have embraced a 'weak' interpretation of TBLT, arguing that while focus on form activities do not constitute tasks in their own right, they do have a place in any task-based instructional cycle. I renewed some of the theoretical and empirical work introduced in Chapter 4 before looking in detail at the issue of focused/

unfocused tasks and consciousness-raising tasks. I then looked at some examples of focus on form being used in the instructional cycle.

References

Doughty, C. and J. Williams (eds) 1998. *Focus on Form in Classroom Second Language Acquisition*. Cambridge: Cambridge University Press.

Ellis, R. 2001. *Task-based Language Teaching and Learning*. Oxford: Oxford University Press.

Ellis, R. 2003. *Task-based Language Learning and Teaching*. Oxford: Oxford University Press.

Gibbons, J. 1989. Instructional cycles. *English Teaching Forum*, 27, 3, 6–11.

Krashen, S. 1981. *Second Language Acquisition and Second Language Learning*. Oxford: Pergamon Press.

Krashen, S. 1982. *Principles and Practice in Second Language Acquisition*. Oxford: Pergamon.

Lantolf, J. (ed.) 2000. *Sociocultural Theory and Second Language Learning*. Oxford: Oxford University Press.

Loschky, L. and R. Bley-Vroman. 1993. Grammar and task-based methodology. In G. Crookes and S. Gass (eds) *Tasks and Language Learning*. Clevedon, Avon: Multilingual Matters.

Nunan, D. 2000. *Go For It: Student book 4*. Singapore: Thomson Learning / People's Education Press.

Nunan, D. 2001. *Expressions: Student book 1*. Boston MA: Heinle / Thomson Learning.

Nunan, D. 2003. *Go For It: Student book 1*. (China edition.) Boston MA: Heinle / Thomson Learning.

Richards, J., J. Hull and S. Proctor. 1997. *New Interchange: English for International Communication. Student's book 1*. Cambridge: Cambridge University Press.

Samuda, V. 2001. Guiding relationships between form and meaning during task performance: the role of the teacher. In M. Bygate, P. Skehan and M. Swain (eds) *Researching Pedagogic Tasks: Second language learning, teaching and testing*. London: Longman.

Ur, P. 1988. *Grammar Practice Activities*. Cambridge: Cambridge University Press.

Wajnryb, R. 1992. *Classroom Observation Tasks*. Cambridge: Cambridge University Press.

Willis, D. and J. Willis. 2001. Task-based language learning. In R. Carter and D. Nunan (eds) *The Cambridge Guide to Teaching English to Speakers of Other Languages*. Cambridge: Cambridge University Press.

6 Grading, sequencing and integrating tasks

Introduction and overview

In this book, I have made the claim that 'task' is more than a methodological device for classroom action, that it is a central curriculum planning tool. In Chapter 1, I argued that curriculum planning embraced the *what*, the *why*, the *when* and the *how well* of any language program. Tasks must therefore feature in decisions relating to each of these dimensions of the curriculum.

I have already devoted a considerable portion of this book to issues of task selection. In this chapter, I want to explore principles for grading, sequencing and integrating tasks.

If you examine a number of coursebooks, you will find that the content is graded in a variety of ways. The grammatical list in one popular coursebook, for example, introduces 'subject pronouns' and 'the verb "be"' in Unit 1, and relegates 'regular past simple', 'possessive pronouns', and 'adjectives' to Unit 9. In another, the functions 'opinions' and 'arguments' are introduced in Unit 3 while 'explanations' and 'instructions' are not introduced until Unit 8. Decisions on what to teach first, what second, and what last in a coursebook or program will reflect the beliefs of the coursebook writer or syllabus designer about grading, sequencing and integrating content. In commercial materials, it will also reflect the demands of the market.

Grading has been described in the following way:

> the arrangement of the content of a language course or textbook so that it is presented in a helpful way. Gradation would affect the order in which words, word meanings, tenses, structures, topics, functions, skills, etc. are presented. Gradation may be based on the complexity of an item, its frequency in written or spoken English, or its importance for the learner.
>
> (Richards, Platt and Weber 1986: 125)

In other words, the content introduced in Week 1 of a course is selected either because it is considered to be easy, or because it occurs frequently, or because the learner needs it immediately for real-world communication.

113

The grading, sequencing and integrating of content for a language program is an extremely complicated and difficult business, even for syllabus designers who have been doing it for years. It could well be the subject of an entire book, and in this chapter. I will only be able to touch on some of the key issues and factors involved in the process.

The issue is complicated by the fact that language development is an 'organic' process (Nunan 1999). Language items are not isolated entities to be mastered one at a time in a step-by-step fashion. Rather they are integrated, and their acquisition is inherently unstable (Ellis 1994). Learners do not learn one aspect of the language perfectly one at a time. Rather, they acquire partial mastery of numerous items simultaneously. For curriculum developers and materials writers, this means that extensive recycling is required. In addition, research has shown that there is a difference between difficulty as defined in terms of linguistic description and difficulty as defined in terms of learners' ability to acquire a particular linguistic item. Pienemann and Johnston (1987), for example, have demonstrated that, while third person 's' is simple in terms of grammatical description, it is complex in terms of language processing.

If deciding which grammatical items are easy or difficult presents problems, then things become much more complicated once we look at the grading and sequencing of tasks. This is because, in addition to linguistic factors, there are so many other factors to be taken into consideration.

I begin this chapter by considering factors in relation to the key components of input, procedures and the learner. Goals are not dealt with separately because they are closely implicated with procedures, and are, in any case, difficult to deal with without a detailed description of the program they come from.

Grading input

In this section, we look at those factors inherent in reading and listening input that are likely to cause difficulty.

The first thing to consider is the complexity of the input. Here, grammatical factors will be important. All things being equal, a text made up of simple sentences is likely to be simpler than one consisting of non-finite verb constructions and subordination.

> **Reflect**
> What factors make Sentence A below less complex than B?

Sentence A
The boy went home.

Sentence B
Having insufficient money, the boy, who wanted to go to the cinema, went home instead.

However, we need to be cautious when making assumptions about difficulty based on the grammatical features contained in a text. Rewriting texts to make them grammatically simpler can actually make them more difficult to process. Consider the following passages:

Passage A
The students fooled around because the teacher left the room.

Passage B
The teacher left the room. The students fooled around.

Question: Why did the students fool around?

Learners reading the grammatically more complex passage (A) will, all things being equal, find the comprehension question easier to answer than those learners reading passage B. This is because the cause/effect relationship is explicitly marked in passage A by the conjunction 'because', whereas readers of passage B will have to infer the relationship. (And, in fact, psychologists have found that student processing time is longer for comprehension exercises that require inferencing.)

In addition to grammatical complexity, difficulty will be affected by the length of a text, propositional density (how much information is packaged into the text and how it is distributed and recycled), the amount of low-frequency vocabulary, the speed of spoken texts and the number of speakers involved, the explicitness of the information, the discourse structure and the clarity with which this is signalled (for example, paragraphs in which the main point is buried away will probably be more difficult to process than those in which the information is clearly foregrounded in the opening sentence of the paragraph). In addition, it has been found that a passage in which the information is presented in the same chronological order as it occurred in real life is easier to process than one in which the information is presented out of sequence (Brown and Yule 1983).

The amount of support provided to the listener or reader will also have a bearing on textual difficulty. A passage with headings and sub-headings which is supported with photographs, drawings, tables, graphs and so on should be easier to process than one in which there is no contextual support. (I say 'should' advisedly. The extent to which all these factors do promote comprehension needs to be demonstrated empirically.)

Numerous investigations have been conducted into the comprehensibility of modified and unmodified versions of aural and written texts. An early study, by Parker and Chaudron (1987), compared the comprehensibility of a text that had been elaborated rather than simplified. They found that the elaborated text, in which the same content was presented in several ways, did not lead to lower comprehensibility as measured by a cloze test. While the researchers pointed out that more research was needed into the effect of interaction, elaboration and simplification on the comprehensibility of aural and written texts, they did argue in favour of elaboration rather than simplification.

Having an overall schema to make sense of input is also important. The importance of top-down schematic knowledge in facilitating comprehension is illustrated by the following story. (We will look in greater detail at the notion of schema in the next section.)

Reflect
Read the following passage, then close the book and see how much of the story you can recall.

If the balloons popped, the sound wouldn't be able to carry since everything would be too far away from the correct floor. A closed window would prevent the sound from carrying, since most buildings tend to be well insulated. Since the whole operation depends on a steady flow of electricity, a break in the middle of the wire would also cause problems. Of course, the fellow could shout, but the human voice is not loud enough to carry that far. An additional problem is that the wire could break on the instrument. Then there could be no accompaniment to the message. It is clear that the best situation would involve less distance. Then there would be fewer potential problems. With face-to-face contact, the least number of things could go wrong.

(Bransford and Johnson 1972: 717).

Most people have a great deal of difficulty remembering much of the story at all.

The story was used in a well-known experiment by two psychologists who found that subjects who heard the story as it appears above understood very little. However, subjects who were given an accompanying visual that provided a context were able to reconstruct a coherent version of the story. The picture showed a man serenading his girlfriend on an electric guitar. The girl was in a high-rise apartment, and the man got his message to her by suspending a loud-speaker from a bunch of balloons.

Another factor that has an impact on processing difficulty is the type or 'genre' of text (Hammond and Derewianka 2001). Genre theorists argue, for example, that narratives, recounts and descriptive texts will be easier to process than abstract or argumentative texts involving the expression of opinions and attitudes.

Reflect
Compare the following passages from Robinson (1977: 80, 118, 129 and 121) and rank them according to their likely difficulty for elementary level readers. Can you identify which features or characteristics (i.e. vocabulary, grammar, genre, etc.) are responsible for text difficulty, or do these various features interact to cause difficulty?

PASSAGE A
The boy felt his way up the creaking stairs through thick darkness, his eyes raised to the faint moonlight that shone along the landing. He stopped as the great clock below whirred for a few seconds and gave out a single solemn stroke. He hesitated as the sound died down and then crept on, thinking if they could sleep through that, they would sleep through any noise he could make. All he had to do was get past that central door on the landing: he was just telling himself he was safe when the door was flung open and the gaunt old man grabbed him by the shoulder.

PASSAGE B
Sound travels at 760 miles per hour, and in the early years of aviation it must have seemed to many that aircraft would always be confined to sub-sonic speeds by the inexorable laws of nature. However, aircraft speed was increased by constant improvements, until, shortly after the Second World War, the first aircraft were built which were capable of speeds faster than that of sound. High speeds presented designers with problems of three kinds, which had to be solved before regular supersonic flights could be considered feasible.

PASSAGE C
Redundancy is a pattern of increasing concern to managers and to professional people who work for companies. The complexity of modern industry means that 'executives' now constitute a larger proportions of a firm's population than before, so that reorganization of management structures make their jobs more precarious than they were in the past. Financial compensation for redundancy is provided under the law, but money does not compensate for the satisfaction that many such people

get from their work and of which redundancy deprives them so that they have considerable problems to face. There are of course wide differences among redundant managers in personality, age, social and family background and reemployment prospects, so that individuals react in varying ways, but few go through the experience with equanimity and for most it is an ordeal.

PASSAGE D
'The Game is Forever' by Jonathan Frost at the Minuscule Theatre. Last night's first night of Mr Frost's play at the Minuscule was a memorable event in my career as a critic, setting new records in the simulation of foot-shuffling and eye rolling, in the production of groans, both suppressed and uttered, and in the intensity of desire it engendered to quit the scene of torture. But I must be calm; it's all over now, the threat implied in the title was mercifully not fulfilled, and it is my duty to tell you what happened. A good deal, indeed far too much, was said and done on the stage last night, but nothing can be said to have happened.

While these passages have all been taken from the same book, they are not all of the same order of difficulty. Not only do they vary in terms of linguistic complexity (for example in terms of grammar and vocabulary), but they also vary in terms of topic and text type. As we know from genre theory, the latter has an important bearing on difficulty (Hammond and Derewianka 2001).

In considering topic, it is generally assumed that abstract topics such as 'redundancy' will pose greater challenges for the reader than more concrete topics such as 'speed' or 'advertising'. However, the extent of the challenge will depend partly on the learner's background knowledge of the topic in question. A text on an unfamiliar concrete topic may well be more challenging than a text on a familiar abstract topic.

This raises the issue of learner factors, and it is to these that we now turn.

Learner factors

In a classic book on reading comprehension, Pearson and Johnson (1972) distinguish between what they call 'inside the head' factors and 'outside the head' factors. 'Inside the head' factors are all those that the learner brings to the task of processing and producing language such as background knowledge, interest, motivation and other factors that we look at below. Pearson and Johnson argue that comprehension is a process of building bridges between the known and the unknown. In other words, we bring to the comprehension process our pre-existing knowledge, and try to fit new knowledge into this pre-existing framework. In those cases where the new knowledge will not fit into our pre-existing framework, we will have to either modify and adapt the framework, or develop an entirely new mental framework altogether.

We can illustrate this as follows. When reading or listening to a story set in a restaurant, we will call up our mental restaurant 'map' to help us understand the story. The restaurant has been constructed from past restaurant experiences. If these experiences have been confined to four-star restaurants, and the story we are reading is set in a fast food restaurant, we may have difficulty comprehending some of the things going on – why, for example, customers go directly to a food counter to place their order rather than having it taken by a waiter. After reading the story, we may have to alter our 'restaurant' framework to accommodate new information. Alternatively, we may need to create a new framework for fast food restaurants.

In learning another language and functioning in an unfamiliar cultural context, we will have to do this constantly. Here is an anecdote that illustrates the cultural significance of knowledge frameworks.

> When I was in Taiwan, I went out to this restaurant for a business dinner with maybe five or six people, and I was the least important person. There was the manager of our Asian office, a local sales representative, and a few other important people. Our host offered me a seat, and I took it, and everyone looked sort of uncomfortable, but no one said anything. But I could tell somehow I had done something wrong. And by Western standards I really didn't feel I had. I simply sat down in the seat I was given. I knew I had embarrassed everyone, and it had something to do with where I was sitting, but I didn't know what it was. . . . Towards the end of the evening, our Asian manager in Taiwan said, 'Just so that you know, you took the seat of honor, and you probably shouldn't have.' And I thought to myself, 'Well, what did I do wrong?' And I asked her, and she said, 'Well, you took the seat that was facing the door, and in Taiwan, that's the seat that's reserved for the most important person in the party, so that if the seat is offered to you, you should decline it. You should decline it several times, and perhaps on the fourth or fifth time that someone insists that you sit there as the foreign guest, you should, but you shouldn't sit there right away, as you did.'

(Nunan 1997)

In this situation, the person applied his Western restaurant knowledge framework which says that when you are offered a seat by a host you take it. However, in many Eastern contexts, this is the wrong thing to do, as the person in the preceding anecdote discovered to his discomfort. However, the experience would have led him to modify his restaurant framework. Seen in this way, even relatively uncomfortable learning experiences can be enriching.

Brindley (1987) suggests that, in addition to background knowledge, learner factors will include confidence, motivation, prior learning experience, learning pace, observed ability in language skills, cultural knowledge / awareness and linguistic knowledge. He proposes a list of questions that need to be considered in relation to each of these factors.

Factor	Question
Confidence	• How confident does the learner have to be to carry out the task? • Does the learner have the necessary level of confidence?
Motivation	• How motivating is the task?
Prior learning experience	• Does the task assume familiarity with certain learning skills? • Does the learner's prior learning experience provide the necessary learning skills/strategies to carry out the task?
Learning pace	• How much learning material has the learner shown he/she is capable of handling? • Is the task broken down into manageable parts?
Observed ability in language skills	• What is the learner's assessed ability in the skills concerned? • Does this assessment conform to his/her observed behaviour in class? • In the light of the teacher's assessment, what overall level of performance can reasonably be expected?
Cultural knowledge/ awareness	• Does the task assume cultural knowledge? • If so, can the learner be expected to have it? • Does the task assume knowledge of a particular subject?
Linguistic knowledge	• How much linguistic knowledge does the learner have? • What linguistic knowledge is assumed by the task?

Adapted from Brindley 1987.

> **Reflect**
> Which of these factors do you think are most likely to be of relevance when considering task difficulty in relation to your own students? Select the three factors that you think are most important when selecting learning tasks, say why they're important, and indicate how you would take them into consideration in selecting and sequencing tasks.

One of the implications of the preceding discussion is that input factors and learner factors are interdependent. For example, there will be an interaction between the grammatical complexity of the input and the learner's linguistic knowledge. The problem for the teacher or materials developer comes in trying to estimate just how much linguistic and background knowledge the learner is likely to have. In relation to reading comprehension, for example, Pearson and Johnson (1972: 10) captured the dilemma as follows:

> [there is an interdependence] between inside the head and outside the head factors. Text readability really boils down to linguistic factors like word difficulty (how familiar are the words?) and sentence complexity (how difficult is it to wade through coordinated and subordinated text segments?). Hence, one cannot know how difficult a text will be until and unless one knows something about the linguistic and conceptual sophistication of the reader: one person's *Scientific American* is another person's daily newspaper. In short, all these factors interact with one another.

To make things even more complex, there is an interaction between the linguistic and content (including cultural) knowledge of readers and listeners as they process written and spoken language (Rost 2002). Second language learners can compensate for lack of linguistic knowledge by drawing on their content knowledge. Conversely, if they lack appropriate background content knowledge, this will adversely affect their ability to mobilize their linguistic knowledge appropriately. In a study carried out some years ago, it was found that lack of appropriate content knowledge had a more significant adverse effect on the ability of secondary ESL students to comprehend school texts than lack of linguistic knowledge (Nunan 1993, 1999). Of course, both are important, but teachers of ESL students can help learners by integrating both linguistic and content instruction, rather than by teaching these separately (see the section below on content-based instruction). The problem for the teacher and textbook writer wanting to accommodate learners' content knowledge is how to estimate just what the learners do or do not know.

> **Reflect**
> How would you estimate the extent of your learners' content knowledge?

Procedural factors

The final set of factors to be considered are those to do with procedures, that is, the operations that learners are required to perform on input data. With the increasing use of authentic texts, the trend has been to control difficulty, not by simplifying the input data but by varying the difficulty level of the procedures themselves. This principle of holding the input constant, but varying the difficulty of the procedures, is illustrated with the following extract from a recently published listening series.

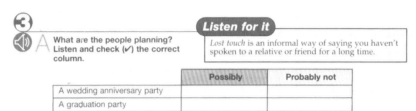

A. What are the people planning? Listen and check (✔) the correct column.

Listen for it
Lost touch is an informal way of saying you haven't spoken to a relative or friend for a long time.

	Possibly	Probably not
A wedding anniversary party		
A graduation party		
An engagement party		
A birthday party		

B. Listen again. Are these people invited or not? Circle the correct answer and write the reason.

Guest	Invited?	Reason
Uncle Ferdie	Yes / Not sure / No	
The Homans	Yes / Not sure / No	
Cousin Henry	Yes / Not sure / No	

We could get him a tie.   **17**

(Nunan 2003: 17)

> **Reflect**
> Do you agree that the second set of procedures is more difficult than the first? What are the factors determining ease and difficulty here?

The two procedures here exploit the same piece of listening material: a discussion between a number of individuals who are planning a social family event. However, the second is much more challenging than the first. The first requires only a very general understanding of the text, whereas the second requires detailed aural processing, and the extraction of a considerable amount of information.

The following factors will determine the complexity of what the learners have to do. They have been adapted from a number of sources including Brindley 1987. (See also Candlin 1987; Nunan 1999; Skehan 1998 and Robinson 2001, as well as the prior discussion in Chapter 3.)

Factor	Question
Relevance	• Is the task meaningful and relevant to the learner?
Complexity	• How many steps are involved in the task? • How complex are the instructions? • What cognitive demands does the task make on the learner? • How much information is the learner expected to process in performing the task?
Amount of context provided prior to the task	• How much prior knowledge of the world, the situation or the cultural context is assumed in the way the task is framed? • How much preliminary activity is allowed for in order to introduce the task and set the context?
Processibility of language of the task	• Is the language that learners are expected to produce in line with their processing capacity? • Can the learners use any language at their disposal, or is the task a 'focused' one requiring deployment of a particular task?

⟫➔

123

Amount of help available to the learner	• How much assistance can the learner get from the teacher, other learners, books or other learning aids? • In the case of interactive tasks, is the interlocutor sympathetic, does he/she provide help?
Degree of grammatical complexity	• What is his/her tolerance level of non-standard language? • How 'standard' does the task require accuracy/fluency/ learners to be? • What is the desired effect on the interlocutor? • Does he/she demand accuracy, fluency or both? • What degree of complexity is required by the learners?
Time available to the learner	• How long does the learner have to carry out the task? • Is planning and rehearsal time built into the task?
Follow-up	• Is there some kind of follow-up, providing debriefing and feedback?

Applying these factors to the kinds of goal statements set out in Chapter 2, we can generate graded sets of specifications such as those below for beginner, pre-intermediate and intermediate level learners. These can be used in developing graded syllabuses, materials and units of work.

Social and interpersonal language

Beginner	Pre-intermediate	High intermediate
introducing yourself greeting others asking who other people are talking about your family asking and answering questions about where you're from welcoming someone offering, accepting and refusing	discussing plans describing others talking about your interests discussing your vacation plans expressing obligation discussing personal habits talking about past events expressing surprise offering congratulations	varying your conversational style to suit your audience using conversational strategies such as seeking turns and holding the floor narrating anecdotes and personal stories expressing approval and disapproval expressing satisfaction/ dissatisfaction

Informational language

Beginner	Pre-intermediate	High intermediate
asking about and stating prices asking for and giving directions describing procedures ordering food and drink asking for additional information	making reservations following a linked sequence of instructions discussing job experience and education	discussing problems and offering solutions taking and relaying messages reporting what others said expressing obligation

Affective

Beginner	Pre-intermediate	High intermediate
reciting songs and rhymes	identifying someone's emotional state from tone and intonation	listening to / reading imaginative texts for pleasure writing short, imaginative text

For further exemplification of graded tasks for the macroskills, see Appendix D.

Task continuity

The terms 'continuity', 'dependency' and 'chaining' all refer to the same thing: the interdependence of tasks, task components and supporting enabling skills within an instructional sequence. In Chapter 2, I introduced one such procedure – one that I use as my 'default option' when planning instructional sequences for general English programs with a four-skills focus.

Another alternative is the 'psycholinguistic processing' approach. This approach sequences tasks according to the cognitive and performance demands made upon the learner. The following steps in a possible instructional sequence require learners to undertake activities which become increasingly demanding, moving from comprehension-based procedures to controlled production activities and exercises, and finally to ones requiring authentic communicative interaction.

Phases	Steps within phase
A. Processing (comprehension)	1. Read or study a text – no other response required. 2. Read or listen to a text and give a non-verbal, physical response (e.g. learner raises hand every time key words are heard). 3. Read or listen to a text and give a non-physical, non-verbal response (e.g. check-off a box or grid every time key words are heard). 4. Read or listen to a text and give a verbal response (e.g. write down key words every time they are heard).
B. Productive	5. Listen to cue utterances, or dialogue fragments and repeat them, or repeat a complete version of the cue. 6. Listen to a cue and complete a sub-stitution or transformation drill. 7. Listen to a cue (e.g. a question) and give a meaningful response (i.e. one that is true for the learner).
C. Interactive	8. Role play (e.g. having listened to a conversation in which people talk about their family, students, working from role cards, circulate and find other members of their family). 9. Simulation/discussion (e.g. students in small groups share information about their own families). 10. Problem-solving / information gap (e.g. in an information gap task, students are split into three groups; each group listens to an incomplete description of a family; students recombine and have to complete a family tree, identify which picture from a number of alternatives represents the family, etc.).

In this ten-step sequence, the demands on the learner gradually increase, both within each phase, and from one phase to the next. The sequence provides yet another illustration of task-chaining or continuity, in that skills acquired and practised in one step are extended in succeeding steps.

126

> **Reflect**
> Create an instructional sequence based on the above three-stage procedure.

One of the earliest and most exciting projects based on the concept of task chaining or continuity was the *Challenges* project developed in Europe in the early days of the communicative language teaching 'revolution'. I have included it here, however, not as an historical 'relic' but because the principles are as relevant today as when the approach was devised. In this approach, tasks were sequenced not only according to their complexity as determined by input, learner and procedural factors, but also by the logic of themes and learning pathways. By allowing learners a range of alternative pathways that matched their needs and interests, the pedagogy enabled a degree of individualization unusual in commercial products. The organization of activity chains in each learning module is described in the following way:

> Thematically, the Chains in each Module each handle one aspect of the view taken under the Unit Theme of that Module. If there are five Chains, for example, in a Module, the learners will have the opportunity (if they want to) to work through five different ways of looking at that general view of the theme. But remember, here there is no rule that says that all the Chains in a given Module have to be worked through.
>
> Let us take an example from SOMETHING TO SAY, the Module titled: WAYS TO SAY IT. There are *six* Chains in this Module and as a result *six* aspects of the Module view of the theme:
>
> A: Slanted information in the mass media. Sorting out facts from opinion.
> B: The idea of a community newspaper *Lower Down*.
> C: How to get your ideas across in public: slogans and speeches.
> D: How to find out what other people think about a problem: using questionnaires.
> E: How to get your opinion across in public: writing to newspapers.
> F: Who do we talk to, and what do we talk about.
> G: How to search for information. Using study skills to broaden your knowledge.
>
> Hopefully you can see how the Chains attack the theme in different ways and how you might become involved in the theme through different *entry points*. Organisationally and pedagogically, the Chains provide a framework for a series of skill steps leading up to a more complex communicative activity, a *Task*. Here is an

example from Chain b of the first Module in the unit SOME-
WHERE TO LIVE.

Step 1: Learners listen to a taped telephone conversation in which
the line is bad and the participants constantly have to use language
which shows that they have not heard correctly what the other
person said. As a result they often have to repeat what they said,
and, in doing so, they express their meaning in a different way.
Step 2: Learners can do a true/false exercise to make sure that they
have caught the gist of the conversation on the telephone.
Step 3: Learners can then do a listening and note-taking exercise in
which they note down the ways in which the speakers showed that
they had not heard, and the ways in which they repeated what
they had to say.
Step 4: Learners are then given a partial or 'defective' dialogue in
the form of a telephone conversation of the same kind as they have
experienced. Here, they can make use of expressions for *'showing
you haven't heard'*, and *'reporting things'* which they have noted
down.

(Candlin and Edelhoff 1982: 26)

Within-task sequencing: the information gap

In the preceding section, we looked at some of the options for sequencing tasks within an instructional cycle. In this section, I would like to
shift the lens down a little to look at procedural sequences *within* a task.
I have chosen to illustrate these points with reference to a common communicative task type, the information gap, but the points could apply to
other task types as well.

The standard way of dividing any mini-sequence is into three phases:
a pre-task phase, a task-proper phase and a follow-up phase. The pre-
task phase fulfils a similar function as schema-building tasks in larger
instruction sequences. It orients the learners to the task, generates interest, and rehearses essential language that will be required to complete the
task. In the task-proper phase learners complete the task. In the follow-
up phase they get a debriefing from the teacher, report the results of the
task back to the class as a whole, and may receive corrective feedback
from the teacher. This phase may also act as a segue into the pre-task
phase of the next task cycle.

> **Reflect**
> Design a pre-task and a follow-up to the following task. Before
> doing so, identify the functions and structures to be elicited by the
> task. If possible, share these with one or two other people and note
> similarities and differences of approach.

Student A

A Look at the activities in the chart. Which are related to work and
which are not?

	Friday evening	Saturday afternoon	Saturday evening	Sunday afternoon	Sunday evening
Bob	Work late	_____	Meet boss at airport	_____	Prepare for a meeting
Karen	_____	Free	_____	Go shopping	_____
Philip	Free	_____	Free	_____	Free
Joan	_____	Take car to garage	_____	Bake cookies	_____

B You and your partner want to go and see a movie with your friends.
Ask questions and decide the best time to go.

C Change one thing about each person's schedule. Do task B again.

Student B

A Look at the activities in the chart. Which are related to work and
which are not?

	Friday evening	Saturday afternoon	Saturday evening	Sunday afternoon	Sunday evening
Bob	_____	Go to meeting	_____	Free	_____
Karen	Clean apartment	_____	Go to visit aunt in in hospital	_____	Free
Philip	_____	Play tennis	_____	Study for exam	_____
Joan	Free	_____	Go to concert	_____	Free

129

B You and your partner want to go and see a movie with your friends. Ask questions and decide the best time to go.

C Change one thing about each person's schedule. Do task B again.

As already indicated, this is an information gap task. Students work in pairs and have access to different information. Student A looks at the first grid and student B looks at the second grid. The grids are on different pieces of paper so that A does not know what information B has and vice versa. Bob, Karen, Philip and Joan are their friends. The task generates language such as the following:

A: What's Karen doing on Friday evening?
B: She has to clean her apartment. What's Bob doing?
A: He's working late.

Once the grid is filled in they decide which time is best because most people are free.

Here is one possible procedure.

Pre-task

A Number the questions and answers to make a conversation (1–6)
Carol: [   ] Oh no, I forgot. I have to work late tonight.
Pete: [   ] Do you want to go to a concert tonight?
Pete: [   ] The Screamers.
Carol: [   ] Hi Pete.
Carol: [   ] Who's playing?
Pete: [   ] Hello Carol.

B Check your answers.

C Practise the conversation with a partner. Then practise again using your own information.

The information gap task practises 'invitations' and 'making plans', and 'making excuses' as well as 'go to' / 'have to'. The pre-task rehearses this language in a controlled and then slightly less controlled way.

Follow-up

A Make a note of the things you have to do this week. Leave two spaces free.

	Monday	Tuesday	Wednesday	Thursday	Friday
Afternoon					
Evening					

B Talk to several other students and arrange a time to see a movie. You might need to change your schedule.

Topic-based / theme-based instruction

In Chapter 2, I discussed the use of topics and themes as the organizing principle for task-based syllabuses. In that chapter, I used the example of 'the neighbourhood', and showed how this enabled the various elements in the task framework to be fitted together. When developing curricula for general English programs, I tend to favour a topic/theme-based approach because it affords maximum flexibility and allows me to bring in a wide variety of content that can be tailored to learner needs. In more specific-purpose course design, I tend to favour variations on content-based instruction.

Content-based instruction

Content-based instruction (CBI) has been popular in certain parts of the world for many years. Despite variations, the thing that unites different approaches to CBI is that the point of departure for syllabus design and materials development is derived from experiential content rather than linguistic criteria. They therefore fit squarely within the 'analytical' rather than 'synthetic' syllabus tradition (Wilkins 1976). This content may come from other subjects on the school curriculum, such as science, history, environmental studies, or it might be generated from an analysis of students' interests and needs.

One of the first people to develop a comprehensive framework for CBI was Mohan (1986). He justified the use of CBI on the grounds that it facilitated learning not merely through language but with language:

> We cannot achieve this goal if we assume that language learning
> and subject-matter learning are totally separate and unrelated
> operations. Yet language and subject matter are still standardly
> considered in isolation from each other.
>
> (Mohan 1986: *iii*)

Content-based instruction has several benefits, all of which are in accord
with the general thrust of other analytical approaches introduced in this
book. In the first place, it is underpinned by the organic, analytical
approach to language development advocated here. Secondly, it can help
school learners master other aspects of school learning in addition to language, and it does so in an integrated way. Thirdly, it provides a framework within which learners can have sustained engagement on both
content mastery and second language acquisition (Murphy and Stoller
2001). For all these reasons, it can raise motivation and heighten the
engagement of the learner in his or her own learning process.

Brinton (2003) sets out five principles for CBI. These are summarized
in the following table.

Principle	Comment
Base instructional decisions on content rather than language criteria.	Content-based instruction allows the choice of content to dictate or influence the selection and sequencing of language items.
Integrate skills.	CBI practitioners use an integrated skills approach to language teaching, covering all four language skills as well as grammar and vocabulary. This reflects what happens in the real world, where interactions involve multiple skills simultaneously.
Involve students actively in all phases of the learning process.	In CBI classrooms, students learn through doing and are actively engaged in the learning process; they do not depend on the teacher to direct all learning or to be the source of all information.
Choose content for its relevance to students' lives, interests and / or academic goals.	The choice of content in CBI courses ultimately depends on the student and the instructional set-tings. In many school contexts, content-based language instruction closely parallels school subjects. ⟫→

132

Select authentic texts and tasks.	A key component of CBI is authenticity – both of the texts used in the classroom and the tasks that the learners are asked to perform.

> **Reflect**
> Select a unit of work from a school or college textbook and design an instructional sequence integrating content and language.

Project-based instruction

Project-based instruction has a great deal in common with the two preceding approaches. Projects can be thought of as 'maxi-tasks', that is a collection of sequenced and integrated tasks that all add up to a final project. For example, a simulation project such as 'buying a new car,' might include the following subsidiary tasks:

1. Evaluating available options and selecting a suitable model based on price, features and so on.
2. Selecting an appropriate car firm from a series of classified advertisements.
3. Arranging for a bank loan through negotiation with a bank or finance house.
4. Role-playing between purchaser and salesperson for purchase of the car.

Ribe and Vidal (1993) argue that project-based instruction has evolved through three 'generations' of tasks. (Slightly confusingly, they tend to use the terms 'project' and 'task' interchangeably.) First-generation tasks focus primarily on the development of communicative ability. These are similar to tasks as they have been conventionally defined in this book.

Example of a first-generation task

Problem-solving
The students have a map with bus and underground routes. They discuss and select the best route for going from one point to another according to a set of given variables (price, time, distance, comfort, etc.)

(Ribe and Vidal 1993: 2)

Second-generation tasks are designed to develop not only communicative competence but also cognitive aspects of the learner as well. They thus incorporate a learning strategies dimension, developing thinking skills, cognitive strategies for handling and organizing information and so on.

Example of a second-generation task

> **Through foreigners' eyes**
> The objective of this task is to collect and analyse information on what tourists of different nationalities think of the students' country/city/town.
>
> 1. Students decide (a) what they need to know; (b) how to get the information (interviews, questionnaires, tourist brochures, etc.); (c) where to get the information (airport, beach, library, tourist information office, etc.); (d) when to obtain the information; (e) what grids / database format they want to use to collate the information; (f) the kind of questionnaires/interviews they want to devise; (g) the language they need to carry out the interviews.
> 2. Students carry out the research, transcribe the interviews and put the information together.
> 3. Students select relevant data, decide on a format (posters, dossier, etc.) for their presentation.
> 4. Students make a report and present it.
>
> (Ribe and Vidal 1993: 11)

Just as second-generation tasks incorporate the characteristics of first-generation tasks, so third-generation tasks incorporate the characteristics of first- and second-generation tasks. In addition to fostering communicative competence and cognitive development, they also aim at personality development through foreign language education. 'Third-generation tasks fulfill wider educational objectives (attitudinal change and motivation, learner awareness, etc.) and so are especially appropriate for the school setting, where motivation for the learning of the foreign language needs to be enhanced.'

⨠→

Example of a third-generation task

Designing an alternative world

1. Students and teachers brainstorm aspects of their environment they like and those they would most like to see improved. These may include changes to the geographical setting, nature, animal-life, housing, society, family, leisure activities, politics, etc.
2. Students are put into groups according to common interests. The groups identify the language and information they need. The students carry out individual and group research on selected topics. The students discuss aspects of this 'alternative reality' and then report back. They decide on the different ways (stories, recordings, games, etc.) to link all the research and present the final product.
3. Students present the topic and evaluate the activity.

(Ribe and Vidal 1993: 2)

Projects, then, are integrated 'maxi-tasks' that could last over the course of a semester, or even over a year. A project can either constitute the main element of instruction to a foreign language class, or run in parallel with more traditional instructions. Regardless of how it fits into the curriculum, Ribe and Vidal (1993) recommend the following ten-step sequence for implementing project-based instruction.

1. create a good class atmosphere
2. get the class interested
3. select the topic
4. create a general outline of the project
5. do basic research around the topic
6. report to the class
7. process feedback
8. put it all together
9. present the project
10. assess and evaluate the project.

Conclusion

In this chapter, I have explored some of the key factors involved in grading, sequencing and integrating tasks. As we have seen, there are many factors determining task difficulty, and deciding on the appropriate ordering of tasks is, in some cases, a matter of trial and error. In addition to the number of factors to be taken into consideration, there is also the issue that the factors themselves are interrelated. Thus, the difficulty of a task based on a relatively simple input text can be increased by adjusting the procedural demands on the learners rather than by changing the input.

In the second part of the chapter, I looked at some proposals for sequencing and integrating tasks, including topic/theme-based, content-based and project-based instruction. Although the suggestions made here are by no means exhaustive, they serve to demonstrate the ways in which tasks can be sequenced and integrated with other activity and exercise types.

References

Bransford, J. and M. Johnson. 1972. Contextual prerequisites for understanding: Some investigations of comprehension and recall. *Journal of Verbal Learning and Verbal Recall*, 11, 717–26.

Brindley, G. 1987. Factors affecting task difficulty. In D. Nunan (ed.) *Guidelines for the Development of Curriculum Resources*. Adelaide: National Curriculum Resource Centre.

Brinton, D. 2003. Content-based instruction. In D. Nunan (ed.) *Practical English Language Teaching*. New York: McGraw Hill.

Brown, G. and G. Yule. 1983. *Teaching the Spoken Language*. Cambridge: Cambridge University Press.

Candlin, C. 1987. Toward task-based learning. In C. Candlin and D. Murphy (eds) *Language Learning Tasks*. Englewood Cliffs NJ: Prentice-Hall.

Candlin, C. and C. Edelhoff. 1982. *Challenges: Teacher's book*. London: Longman.

Ellis, R. 1994. *The Study of Second Language Acquisition*. Oxford: Oxford University Press.

Hammond, J. and B. Derewianka. 2001. Genre. In R. Carter and D. Nunan (eds) *The Cambridge Guide to TESOL*. Cambridge: Cambridge University Press.

Mohan, B. 1986. *Language and Content*. Reading MA: Addison-Wesley.

Murphy, J. and F. Stoller. 2001. Sustained-content language teaching: An emerging definition. *TESOL Journal*, 10, 2–3.

Nunan, D. 1993. *Introducing Discourse Analysis*. London: Penguin.

Nunan, D. 1997. *ATLAS: Learning-Centered Communication. Level 3 Student's Book*. Boston MA.: Heinle / Thomson.

Nunan, D. 1999. *Second Language Teaching and Learning*. Boston MA.: Heinle and Heinle.

Nunan, D. 2003. *Listen: Student book 3*. Boston MA: Heinle and Heinle.

Parker, K. and C. Chaudron. 1987. The effects of linguistic simplification and elaborative modifications on L2 comprehension. *The University of Hawaii Working Papers in ESL*, 6, 2, 107–133.

Pearson, P. D. and D. D. Johnson. 1972. *Teaching Reading Comprehension*. New York: Holt, Rinehart and Winston.

Pienemann, M. and M. Johnston. 1987. Factors affecting the development of language proficiency. In D. Nunan (ed.) *Applying Second Language Aquisition Research*. Adelaide, National Curriculum Resource Centre.

Robinson, C. 1977. *Advanced Use of English: a coursebook*. London: Hamish Hamilton.

Robinson, P. 2001. *Cognition and Second Language Instruction*. Cambridge: Cambridge University Press.

Rost, M. 2002. *Teaching and Researching Listening*. London: Longman.

Ribe, R. and N. Vidal. 1993. *Project Work Step by Step*. Oxford: Heinemann.

Richards, J., J. Platt and H. Weber. 1986. *Longman Dictionary of Applied Linguistics*. London: Longman.

Rudolph, S. 1993. *Project-Based Learning*. Tokyo: Newbury House.

Skehan, P. 1998. *A Cognitive Approach to Language Learning*. Oxford: Oxford University Press.

Wilkins, D. 1976. *Notional Syllabuses*. Oxford: Oxford University Press.

7 Assessing task-based language teaching

Introduction and overview

Task-based language teaching presents challenges in all areas of the curriculum. This is particularly so in the area of assessment. Traditional, language-based curricula provide a convenient basis for the assessment specialist whose point of departure in developing assessment instruments is to provide a representative sampling of the grammar, vocabulary and phonological features of the language. These are then assessed, usually through some indirect form of assessment. While it is always possible to continue using traditional methods to assess students who are learning through task-based teaching, this violates a key curriculum principle, which is that assessment should reflect what has been taught.

Aligning this principle with TBLT makes direct assessment inevitable. An additional problem, as we saw in Chapter 5, is that there is rarely a simple one-to-one correlation between communicative tasks and the linguistic elements through which they are realized (Willis and Willis, 2001).

Understandably, this chapter draws on some of the research summarized in Chapter 4. It also reports on some additional research related specifically to assessment.

Key concepts in assessment

Evaluation versus assessment

In this chapter, I will draw a distinction between evaluation and assessment, two terms which in some contexts are used interchangeably. For me, 'evaluation' is a broad, general set of procedures involving the collection and interpretation of information for curricular decision making. This information will generally include data on what learners can and cannot do in the language. Procedures for collecting this learner data are referred to as 'assessment'. Assessment is thus a subset of evaluation. Testing is one form of assessment. It includes the more formal collection of data on learner performance. In other words, assessment subsumes testing and is, in turn, subsumed by evaluation.

Evaluation can take place at any time, and any aspect of the curriculum can be evaluated. At the beginning of the curriculum planning process, for example, the curriculum developer might design a needs assessment instrument for collecting data. This instrument could be evaluated by, for instance, subjecting it to peer review.

Gronlund (1981) argues that assessment measures need to satisfy three types of validity. These are content validity, criterion-related validity and construct validity, which are summarized in the following table. Each presents particular challenges to the assessment of learner performance in task-based language teaching.

Type	Meaning	Procedure
Content validity	How well does the sample of tasks represent the domain of tasks to be measured?	Compare the test tasks to the test specifications describing the task domain under consideration.
Criterion-related validity	How well does test performance predict future performance or estimate current performance on some valued measures other than the test itself?	Compare test scores with another measure of performance obtained at a later date (for prediction) or with another measure of performance obtained concurrently (for estimating present status).
Construct validity	How can test performance be described psychologically?	Experimentally determine what factors influence scores on the test.

Indirect versus direct assessment

Another important distinction is between indirect and direct assessment. In direct assessment, learners are required to reproduce, in the testing situation, the kinds of communicative behaviours they will need to carry out in the real world. In indirect tests, as the label implies, the test does not resemble outside-class performance.

> **Reflect**
>
> Consider the following assessment items. What are they attempting to measure? What would successful performance tell the teacher and/or the learner? Are the items direct or indirect?

Example 1
Underline the correct word in the parentheses.

Example: You have a headache. You (should / <u>shouldn't</u>) go to the party.

He's hungry. He (should/shouldn't) eat something.
They are very tired. They (should/shouldn't) do strenuous exercise.
You are stressed out. You (should/shouldn't) stay home and relax.
He is stressed out. He (should/shouldn't) talk about homework.
She has a toothache. She (should/shouldn't eat junk food.

Example 2
Match the problem with the advice.

I can't sleep at night.	You should listen to quiet music.
I have a sore throat.	You should see a dentist.
I am stressed out.	You shouldn't go out at night.
I have a headache.	You should see a doctor.
I'm very tired.	You should lie down and rest.
I have a toothache.	You should drink hot tea with honey.

Example 3
Your teacher will ask you five questions from the following list. Be prepared to answer the questions.

1. Are you an exchange student?
2. How do you spell your last name?
3. What's your address?
4. What kind of music do you like?
5. What does your mother (or father/brother/sister) look like?
6. What do you want to be?
7. What does your friend want to be?
8. Did you go to the movies yesterday?
9. Would you like pizza for dinner? What would you like on it?
10. Are you watching TV? What are you doing now?
11. Is your friend very serious? What's your friend like?
12. What did you and your family (or friends) do over the weekend?
13. Are you moody? What are you like?
14. What are you wearing today?
15. How's the weather today?

Example 4
Work with another student. Take turns to be Student A and Student B.

Student A	Student B
1. Ask Student B 'How was your vacation?'	2. Answer Student A.
3. Ask Student B 'Where did you go?'	4. Answer Student A.
5. Ask Student B 'How was the weather?'	6. Answer Student A.
7. Ask Student B 'How long did you stay?'	8. Answer Student A.

(Source: Nunan 1999b)

System-referenced versus performance-referenced tasks

Another important distinction in task-based language testing, and one that is related to the direct/indirect distinction, is that between system-referenced tests and performance-referenced tests (Robinson and Ross 1996). A system-referenced test item requires the candidate to demonstrate knowledge of the phonological, lexical or grammatical systems of the language. It is designed to 'evaluate language mastery as a psychological construct without specific reference to any particular use of it' (Baker 1990: 76). A performance-based item, on the other hand, requires the learner to demonstrate an ability to use the language.

Robinson and Ross (1996: 459) provide the following schematic representation of the relationship between the concepts of direct and indirect tests and system versus performance-referencing.

Mode	System-referenced	Performance-referenced
Direct	Sample of oral or written language via interview and/or composition	Communicative simulation of target tasks, e.g. library skills, reading test
Indirect	Grammar and reading multiple-choice tests	Breakdown of simulation into sub-tasks for multiple-choice formats

The question arises, then, as to why one would use indirect assessment measures in the first place. There are several reasons. In the first place, performance-based assessment, particularly the assessment of speaking, can be difficult to set up and control. Grading learner performance can also be highly problematic. Discrete-point test items such as the ones above, on the other hand, can be quickly and conveniently administered to many learners at the same time. They are also easy to score, and the scoring can often be done automatically. Proponents of indirect assessment argue that, if a high correlation can be shown between an indirect test and communicative performance, the indirect measure is justified.

In arguing for direct, performance-based assessment, Norris *et al.* (1998: 15) point out that the value of such an approach lies in the fact that:

> . . . it measures students' abilities to respond to real-life language tasks. In other words, unlike other types of tests, performance assessments can be used to approximate the conditions of a real task in a real-life situation. As a result, performance assessments have value in that their scores can be used to predict students' abilities in future real-world situations unlike other tests where scores are only very indirect predictors of ability to perform a real-life language task. We suggest that the potential for predicting or generalizing to future, real-world language use is one of the key contributions that performance assessment might make as an alternative form of language assessment.

Assessing proficiency versus achievement

A major challenge for language researchers, including those involved in language testing research, is that the qualities being researched or tested are abstract, invisible psychological qualities such as aptitude, motivation and language proficiency. The only way that we can gather information on these phenomena is through observation or elicitation of some kind of performance on the part of the learner. Thus, we administer a test of general language proficiency, and then, based on the results, infer that Student X is at an 'upper-intermediate level of proficiency', while Student Y is at a 'false beginning level of proficiency'.

This dilemma for testers, inferring invisible qualities from performance, has been captured by Ingram (1984: 10–11) as follows:

> . . . language occurs only in situations, and, if proficiency descriptions are related to particular situations, one could be accused of measuring only proficiency in specific situations, i.e. one would not be measuring general proficiency, but proficiency in specific situations. On the other hand, language varies from situation to situation; it varies according to who is using it, to whom, and about what subject . . . in other words, it would seem as though one cannot speak of general proficiency so much as proficiency in a language in this situation or that, in this register or that. Yet such a view would seem to be counter-intuitive. If we say that X speaks Chinese . . . we do not mean that X can only give a lecture on

> engineering in Chinese. . . . Rather, when we say that someone can
> speak a language, we mean that that person can speak the
> language in the sorts of situations people commonly encounter. . . .
> General proficiency, then, refers to the ability to use the language
> in these everyday, non-specific situations.

Brindley (1989) draws a distinction between the assessment of proficiency, as defined by Ingram, and the assessment of achievement. While
proficiency is meant to be independent of any particular course of study,
achievement refers to the mastery by the learner of specific curricular
objectives. Proficiency is typically assessed by rating students on a proficiency rating scale such as the ACTFL scale (see below). Attainment of
curricular objectives can be carried out more informally using a wide
range of instruments including teacher-constructed tests, self-rating
scales, learner self-reports, teacher or learner diaries, and videotaped or
audiotaped samples of learners' work (Brindley 1989: 11).

While the timing and purposes of these two forms of assessment use
different tools, and have different purposes, and while proficiency assessment is meant to be independent of a given syllabus, Brindley argues that
the distinction is increasingly blurred. He points out that if proficiency
is defined in terms of people's ability to use language for particular communicative purposes then it 'can be interpreted as the achievement of the
particular communicative objectives which the target group is likely to
have' (p. 11). He goes on to point out that if this view is accepted, an
end-of-course test derived from course objectives would appear to be
serving the same purposes as a general proficiency test.

Teaching versus testing

Almost any teaching task can be used for assessment purposes, and vice
versa. The key difference is how the task fits into an instructional cycle
and, crucially, what is done with the learner output from the task.

> **Reflect**
> Consider the following teaching task. How might it be modified to
> become a testing task?

PRE-TASK 4   Ordering from a menu

A *Work in pairs. Look at the restaurant menu below. Do you know how to pronounce these words? Take turns to read out the food items and the prices.*

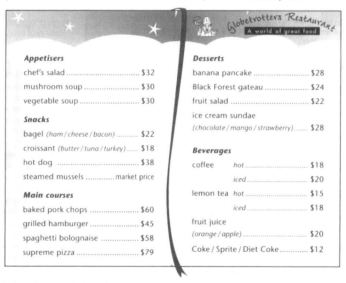

Appetisers

chef's salad $32

mushroom soup $30

vegetable soup $30

Snacks

bagel *(ham / cheese / bacon)* $22

croissant *(butter / tuna / turkey)* $18

hot dog $38

steamed mussels .... market price

Main courses

baked pork chops $60

grilled hamburger $45

spaghetti bolognaise $58

supreme pizza $79

Desserts

banana pancake $28

Black Forest gateau $24

fruit salad $22

ice cream sundae
(chocolate / mango / strawberry) $28

Beverages

coffee   hot $18

            iced $20

lemon tea hot $15

            iced $18

fruit juice
(orange / apple) $20

Coke / Sprite / Diet Coke $12

B *Alan and Danny go to Globetrotters Restaurant and order some food. Listen to what they order and help the waitress to fill in the order form below.*

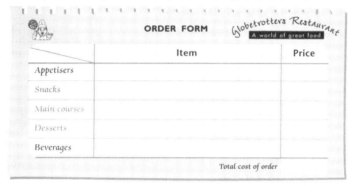

ORDER FORM   Globetrotters Restaurant   A world of great food

	Item	Price
Appetisers		
Snacks		
Main courses		
Desserts		
Beverages		
	Total cost of order	

(Nelson *et al.*, 2001: 72)

144

Task-based assessment

Task-based tests require candidates to perform an activity which simulates a performance they will have to engage in outside the test situation. Performance-based assessment has been around for many years in other fields. For example, in order to obtain a driving licence, it is necessary to demonstrate one's ability by actually driving. Most people would think it odd if such a licence could be obtained simply by taking a pencil and paper test.

Norris *et al.* (1998) argue that task-based testing is part of a broader approach to assessment called performance assessment. There are three essential characteristics of performance assessment. Firstly, it must be based on tasks; secondly, the tasks should be as authentic as possible; and finally, 'success or failure in the outcome of the task, because they are performances, must usually be rated by qualified judges.' (p. 8).

Norris *et al.* develop a set of test specifications for designing and grading tasks. They identify four factors to be taken into consideration in grading tasks: code, cognitive complexity, communicative demand, and overlapping variables. An example of a task-based test item, along with an indication of how task difficulty might be adjusted, is provided below.

Task: Reserving a table

Prompt
You live in the USA and would like to try out the fancy new Italian bistro *Il Gondoliero* tonight. Unfortunately, no one is free to accompany you to dinner (this can be changed to include a dinner partner). Look up the phone number of the restaurant in the phone book and call to reserve a table for one at an appropriate time this evening. You will have to speak with the answering machine as the staff do not come in until 5.00 p.m.

code
low
Phone book layout, where to look (restaurants – could give option of white versus yellow pages, let them choose, white actually being more efficient, alphabetically); comprehension of the message on answering machine and when to begin talking; forms and necessary information for requesting a reservation ('I would like to request a table for one . . .'); time vocabulary, day of the week, evening; sociocultural knowledge about when dinners typically take place in the United States (not 2 a.m.).

⟫▶

Could step up the code with difficult message, heavily accented speech. However, success is pretty generically dependent on examinee knowledge of forms and vocabulary for the situation (as well as cultural knowledge of the situation/task itself); could also add the element of a dinner party (dinner for two).

cognitive complexity

low

Monologic speech with a machine and planning time make it a pretty easy task; ratings could be based to some extent on *efficiency* of execution.

high

Step up demand by introducing an interlocutor on the other end of the line when reserving; likewise, new information introduced through the message could increase demand ('we will be closed this evening for the cook's birthday, but will reopen tomorrow . . .;' 'if you are making a reservation, please indicate smoking preference').

communicative demand

low

One-way task with near total control in examinee; skimming phone book, calling restaurant, understanding machine, making reservation; low pressure, plenty of time.

high

Varied time pressure introduced through message ('you have twenty seconds to leave a message . . .') or through situation (you are phoning from work, so you should make it quick); interlocutor makes it two-way.

(Norris *et al.* 1998: 153)

Norm-referenced versus criterion-referenced assessment

Another important distinction in the assessment literature is that between norm-referenced and criterion-referenced assessment. Both concepts have to do with how student test scores are interpreted (Bailey 1998).

In norm-referenced testing, students are compared to each other. Norm-referenced testing procedures are designed to disperse students' scores along a normal distribution. With this procedure, some students will do very well, the majority will do reasonably well, and some will do quite poorly. According to Brown (1989) and Brown and Hudson (2002: 2), this form of assessment is appropriate for 'assessing abstracted language ability traits'. They cite as examples of such traits overall ESL proficiency, lecture listening ability, and academic reading comprehension. Criterion-referenced tests, on the other hand, compare students, not against each other, but on how well they do on a given assessment task. Potentially, all students might receive an 'A' grading on a criterion-referenced test. (Alternatively, they might all receive an 'F'.)

I believe that criterion-referenced testing is more appropriate than norm-referenced testing in task-based language teaching, particularly in educational systems where there is a concern to achieve a high degree of harmony between teaching and testing. Criterion-referenced tests are designed to assess students' mastery of course objectives. The fact that task-based language teaching and criterion-referenced testing are both concerned with student performance reinforces this natural 'fit', as Glaser and Nitko (1971: 653) attest.

> A criterion-referenced test is one that is deliberately constructed to yield measurements that are directly interpretable in terms of specified performance standards. Performance standards are generally specified by defining a class or domain of tasks that should be performed by the individual.

Brown and Hudson (2002: 9) make a similar case for criterion-referenced testing because of the following characteristics that it can be expected to exhibit:

1. Emphasis on teaching/testing matches.
2. Focus on instructional sensitivity.
3. Curricular relevance.
4. Absence of normal distribution restrictions.
5. No item discrimination restrictions.

The purposes of assessment

The reasons for carrying out assessment in the first place should have an important bearing on how the assessment is carried out, when it is carried out, by whom, and how the results will be reported. An assessment carried out for the purposes of placing students in groups will be very different from one undertaken to provide students with a final grade on their course.

In an investigation carried out in an immigrant education program, Brindley (1989) asked teachers to rate a list of the functions of assessment according to their perceived importance. The results are set out in the following table.

Function of assessment	Mean	Standard deviation	Rank
Place learners in classes	4.296	1.059	1
Provide feedback on progress	3.888	1.221	4
Provide information on learners' strengths and weaknesses for course planning	4.137	1.129	2
Provide information to funding authorities for accountability purposes	2.482	1.512	6
Encourage students to take responsibility for their own learning	3.957	1.268	3
Provide students with a record of their achievement	3.207	1.393	5

Brindley (1989: 24) makes the following comment on these data:

> Placement of learners in classes was, interestingly, considered to be the most important function. Providing information on learners' strengths and weaknesses for course-planning purposes and encouraging students to take responsibility for their own learning were also rated as important. Predictably, providing information for funding authorities for accountability purposes was ranked lowest, with a mean of 2.5. However, this by no means represented a uniform response, since 24 per cent of teachers ranked this function as important or very important, as opposed to 41 per cent who considered it to be of no importance or of low importance.

Reflection
With reference to your own teaching situation, or a teaching situation with which you are familiar, do your own ranking of the items in the above table.

To what extent is your ranking similar to or different from those provided in the Brindley study? How would you account for any difference?

Self-assessment

In addition to assessment by the teacher, self- and peer assessment are also becoming popular. This is particularly true in classrooms where teachers wish to encourage learner autonomy and a focus on learning processes as well as learning outcomes. While self-assessment has been criticized on the grounds that not all learners are accurate judges of their own ability, this criticism misses the point to some extent, which is to involve learners in their own learning processes:

> The major purpose of self-assessment is to provide the opportunity for learners to develop an understanding of their own level of skill, knowledge or personal readiness for a task in relation to their goals. This level will often be compared with a previously deter-mined level and incorporated either into a summative report of gains made during a course or into a cumulative record of learner achievement.
>
> (Cram 1995: 282)

The following self-assessment checklist has been taken from a step-by-step guide to project work. The points can be elaborated, as in 3b.

SELF ASSESSMENT	Student				Teacher				Comment
Objective	0	1	2	3	0	1	2	3	
1 I have co-operated in group work.									
2 I can solve my language problems by consulting grammar books and dictionaries.									
3a I can communicate in English in ordinary classroom situations.									
3b I have made a point of using English when speaking with the teacher and classmates, and have helped my classmates use it.									
I can ask for an explanation of what I do not understand									

149

SELF ASSESSMENT	Student				Teacher				Comment
Objective	0	1	2	3	0	1	2	3	
I can explain what I have done in simple terms.									
I can make suggestions to the group.									
I can give reasons for my decisions.									
4 I can write a simple story in correct English.									
I can use the past tenses (regular and irregular) correctly.									
I can use many different sequencers (e.g. *then, later*, etc.).									
I can use words (especially adverbs) in their correct position in the sentence.									
I can use a range of different words to avoid monotony and make the story entertaining.									

(Ribe and Vidal 1993: 83–4)

Reflect
Consider how this checklist might be incorporated into your own teaching. What modifications would you want to make to it? How and when would you use it? What would you do with the results?

Cram (1995) provides the following matrix of questions that students can address in assessing their language performance. It shows what a rich array of data can be collected, not just on overall language gains, but also on functional and affective gains.

Levels of Achievement	Areas of Achievement			
	General Linguistic	Socio-Cultural	Vocational/ Academic	Learning for Life/ Independent
Proficiency (overall gains)	Have I reached a higher level of proficiency in: • reading • writing • listening • speaking?	Do I 'fit' better into the local sub-culture?	Am I able to cope better in the academic/ vocational area that I plan to pursue?	Have I developed strategies for life-long learning? Am I a more indepen-dent learner?
Practice (functional gains)	Can I carry out (Task X) better? e.g. obtain information by telephone	Do I behave more appropriately in both formal and informal situations?	Can I carry out academic or vocational tasks more effectively? e.g. write a letter using a computer	Have I improved my: • research skills • independent learning skills • ability to diag-nose strengths?
Theory/ Structural (gains in knowledge, understanding)	Have I increased my knowledge of the structure of English? e.g. tenses	Have I increased my knowledge of Australian customs? e.g. gender roles, educational practices	Have I increased my knowledge of educational or vocational practices in this country? e.g. career pathways	Have I increased my knowledge of: • learning strategies • services and how to access them?
Affective (gains in motivation, confidence)	Am I more confident when I use English?	Am I more confident in my social interactions?	Am I more confident that I can achieve my educational/ vocational goals?	Am I more motivated to continue learning independently after the course?

(Cram 1995: 291)

> **Reflect**
> Using Cram's table as a guide, create your own self-assessment questionnaire.

Levels of Achievement	Areas of Achievement			
	General Linguistic	Socio-Cultural	Vocational/ Academic	Learning for Life/ Independent
Proficiency (overall gains)				
Practice (functional gains)				
Theory/ Structural (gains in knowledge, understanding)				
Affective (gains in motivation, confidence)				

(Cram 1995: 292)

152

Techniques for collecting assessment data

There is almost no limit to techniques and procedures for collecting assessment data in task-based language classrooms. In their book on classroom-based evaluation, Genesee and Upshur (1996) introduce observation, portfolios, conferences, journals, questionnaires and interviews as particularly pertinent non-testing tools for evaluation.

Brindley (1989: 169–71) lists the following, many of which could be adapted for task-based assessment:

- observation followed by recycling of work
- informal discussions with learners about their progress
- teacher-constructed classroom tests
- student self-assessment procedures
- teacher journal (teacher writes descriptive account of what happens in class
- learner journal
- oral proficiency rating
- feedback from others outside the classroom (e.g. employers, community organizations)
- Standardized published tests.

Performance scales

Performance scales have been popular tools for direct assessment for many years. Because they are performance based and set out to describe learner behaviour, they are particularly suitable for task-based assessment. Early proficiency scales such as the ACTFL (American Council for Teaching Foreign Languages scale) provided descriptions such as the following for assessing learner performance at different levels. The extract on p. 154 describes performance at intermediate level:

Able to satisfy most survival needs and limited social demands.

Shows some spontaneity in language production, but fluency is very uneven.

Can initiate and sustain a general conversation but has little understanding of the social conventions of conversation.

Developing flexibility in a range of circumstances beyond immediate survival needs.

Limited vocabulary range necessitates much hesitation and circumlocution.

The commoner tense forms occur but errors are frequent in formation and selection.

Can use most question forms.

While some word order is established, errors still occur in more complex patterns.

Cannot sustain coherent structures in longer utterances or unfamiliar situations.

Ability to describe and give precise information is limited.

Aware of basic cohesive features such as pronouns and verb inflections but many are unreliable, especially if less immediate in reference.

Extended discourse is largely a series of short, discrete utterances.

Articulation is comprehensible to native speakers used to dealing with foreigners, and can combine most phonemes with reasonable comprehensibility, but still has difficulty in producing certain sounds in certain positions or in certain combinations, and speech will usually be laboured.

Still has to repeat utterances frequently to be understood by the general public.

Able to produce some narration in either past or future.

(Savignon and Berns 1984: 228–9)

The most recent, and certainly most comprehensive, set of frameworks for assessing learner performance is provided by the Council of Europe (2001). Descriptive scales are provided for global language assessment as well as for specific language skills and strategies. Appendix E provides an example of one of these scales.

Production tasks: role plays, discussion tasks and simulations

As already indicated, practically any pedagogical task can be used for assessing learner progress. The main difference lies in how the task is set up, and how learner language is recorded and analysed. You might want to obtain actual samples of learner language, or, alternatively, to capture aspects of learner–learner interaction. If the latter is the case, then observation schedules such as the one presented in the next section may suffice.

In selecting language production tasks, it is important to be clear about the purpose, as well as the kind of language you want to elicit. Consider the following tasks.

Example1

---

10 ROLE PLAY *Can I help you?*

Student A: You are a customer in a drugstore. You need:

something for a sunburn
something for sore muscles
something for a sore throat

Ask for some suggestions.

Student B: You are a pharmacist in a drugstore. A customer needs some things. Make some suggestions.

a can of sunburn spray   a tube of muscle ointment   a bottle of throat spray

Change roles and try the role play again. Make up your own information.

(Richards et al. 1997: 76)

Example 2

8 Express Yourself

(A) Plan a package tour for people visiting your city for the first time. Include details about sights, transportation, accommodation, restaurants, price, and so on.

_____ Tour

Includes:
_____
_____
_____
_____

Cost:_____

(B) Ask people from other groups about their tours. How are they similar or different?

(C) Return to your own group. Compare the information you collected. Which package is the best value? Which were the most popular items on the tours?

(Nunan 2001: 53)

Assessing task-based language teaching

While the role play and the simulation can both be used to assess learner language, they were initially designed for classroom instruction.

Observation schedules

The number of observation schedules is almost limitless. For an excellent collection of observation tasks, many of which are suitable for collecting assessment data in the task-based classroom, see Wajnryb (1992). The following checklist is intended to assess the ability of students to contribute to small-group discussions in task-based conversation classes.

Indicate the degree to which learners contribute to small-group discussions by circling the appropriate number.

Key:
5 – outstanding
4 – above average
3 – average
2 – below average
1 – unsatisfactory

The learner participates in discussions.	1 2 3 4 5
The learner uses appropriate non-verbal signals.	1 2 3 4 5
The learner's contributions are relevant.	1 2 3 4 5
The learner negotiates meaning.	1 2 3 4 5
The learner conveys factual information.	1 2 3 4 5
The learner gives personal opinions.	1 2 3 4 5
The learner invites contributions from others.	1 2 3 4 5
The learner agrees / disagrees appropriately.	1 2 3 4 5
The learner changes topic appropriately.	1 2 3 4 5

In a learner-centred classroom, it is possible to get learners to generate their own checklists. I do this by showing students three videotaped group discussions, one of which is good, one of which is average, and one of which is mediocre. Students view the videotapes and rank order them from good to poor. They then work in groups to say why one performance was good, and why one was not so good. Based on their discussion, they are then led to articulate a set of criteria for good group discussions. This is then used to evaluate their own performance. In this way assessment becomes part of the learning process.

Journals, diaries and learning logs

Journals, diaries and learning logs can be excellent resources for collecting evidence of student learning. In addition to encouraging learners to become more reflective and self-directed, they can help to bring together teaching and assessment in mutually beneficial ways.

I have used the following proforma successfully with intermediate level learners and above. Each week, the learners complete the sentence starters, and, over the course of a semester, they have a concrete record of their growth and development.

Complete one diary sheet each week

This week I studied ....

This week I learned ....

This week I used my English in these places ....

This week I spoke English with these people ....

This week I made these mistakes ....

My difficulties are ....

I would like to know ....

I would like help with ....

My learning and practising plans for next week are ....

The following table, which provides same learner entries from the beginning and end of a language program, illustrate how much sharper and more perceptive one group of students became as a result of systematically completing a guided journal over a semester.

Probe	At the beginning of the course	At the end of the course
This week I studied:	*The nature of verbs.*	*I read a journal article called Geographic which is published in New Zealand. I have spent an hour in discussion with my psychology classmates.*
This week I learned:	*Some more information about English in English linguistics lesson.*	*The principles of morphology. How to use the self-access centre for learning English.*
This week I used my English in these places:	*Tutorials. My German lesson.*	*In the library, Knowles Building, K.K. Leung Building. At home. Along the street near my home.*
This week I spoke English with these people:	*History lecturer, classmates and tutor, linguistics tutor.*	*A foreigner – he asked me where is Lok Fu MTR station. The waiter in Mario restaurant.*
This week I made these mistakes:	*Using incorrect words.*	*I spent too much time watching TV while answering questions; I created a word 'gesturally'.*
My difficulties are:	*Lack of time.*	*Understanding the theme of a topic or an article. Writing fluent English essays.*
I would like to know:	*How to improve my English.*	*The method that can improve both my listening and speaking skills.*
I would like help with:	*Dictionaries.*	*Ensuring I would spend some time on reading but not on other leisure activities. Communicating with foreigners. Watching foreign films. Human resources that can improve my language ability.*
My learning and practising plans for next week are:	*To talk more.*	*To speak up in class and use English to ask about anything I don't understand in any of my subjects. To try to understand by explaining to my schoolmates some topics of the essay before writing it.*

(Nunan 1996: 41)

Dialogue journals provide a useful record of achievement, although they can be time-consuming for the teacher to read and respond to. With dialogue journals, the teacher reads and responds individually, in writing, to each student's journal entries.

Genesee and Upshur (1996: 123–4) provide the follow guidelines for using dialogue journals.

1. Students should have separate books for journal writing. Students with access to computers may want to keep electronic journals.
2. Set aside regular times – at the end of class or at the beginning or end of the day – when students can write in their journals.
3. Collect students' journals on a regular basis and read them carefully before returning them. Reading journals is time-consuming, so it is important to find a method of keeping track of them that works for you.
4. Writing journals is not easy in the beginning. Students will probably need some direction in order to know what you are looking for.
5. Encourage students to write about their successes as well as their difficulties and hardships. Similarly, encourage them to write about classroom activities and events that they found useful, effective and fun as well as those they found to be confusing, useless, uninteresting or frustrating.
6. Be patient and allow students time to develop confidence in the process of sharing their personal impressions.
7. Avoid the use of evaluative or judgmental comments to ensure students' confidence and candor.
8. Help students interpret their own feedback and decide on actions to take in response to it.

Portfolios

Portfolios are different in kind from the other instruments discussed in this section. They can contain a wide range of written (and also spoken) language data, and can incorporate all of the other instruments already discussed. According to Kemp and Toperoff (1998), student assessment through portfolios should contain the following characteristics:

- The assessment should be a joint endeavour between students and teachers
- The portfolio should not consist of a random collection of samples. Rather, items should be carefully selected and justified.
- Samples of work should show growth and development over time.
- The criteria for selecting and assessing content must be clear to students from the outset.

159

Nunan and Wong (2003) argue that portfolios should contain the following:

1. *A self-introduction*   This provides an introduction and overview as well as a rationale from the author on the exhibits presented in the portfolio.
2. *Samples of both spoken and written language*   For completeness, the portfolio needs to contain samples of both spoken and written language.
3. *Evidence of growth and development*   The exhibits presented in the portfolio should provide clear evidence of growth and development on the part of the student.
4. *Evidence of reflective learning*   In many ways, this is the most important part of the portfolio. It gives the author an opportunity to set out his or her strengths (and weaknesses) as a language learner as well as a statement on what he or she gained from the process of constructing the portfolio.

Kemp and Toperoff (1998: 3–4) list the following advantages of a portfolio:

- Has clear goals: these are decided on at the beginning of instruction and are clear to teacher and students alike.
- Gives a profile of learner abilities.
- Depth: [the portfolio] enables students to show quality work, which is done without pressure and time constraints, and with the help of resources, reference materials and collaboration with others.
- Breadth: a wide range of skills can be demonstrated.
- Growth: it shows efforts to improve and develop, and demonstrates progress over time.
- Assesses a variety of skills: written as well as oral and graphic products can easily be included.
- Develops awareness of own learning: students have to reflect on their own progress and the quality of their work in relation to known goals.
- Caters to individual differences and enhances independent learning: since it is open-ended, students can show work on their own level. Since there is a choice, it caters to different learning styles and allows expression of different strengths.
- Develops social skills: students are also assessed on work done together, in pairs or groups, on projects and assignments.
- Develops independent and active learners: students must select and justify portfolio choices; monitor progress and set learning goals.

These points have in common that they all point to the fact that portfolios provide direct indicators of growth and that they integrate assessment with other aspects of the learning process. In particular, as they are based on the outcomes of classroom work, there is no disjunction between the implemented and the assessed curriculum (Nunan 1988, 1999a) as is often the case with indirect tests.

Criteria for assessing learner performance

Accuracy, fluency and complexity

In Chapter 4, we looked at the work of Skehan (1998) and Skehan and Foster (1999), who proposed three key variables for assessing learner performance: accuracy, complexity and fluency. These researchers found that systematically manipulating the characteristics of tasks resulted in different levels of accuracy, complexity and fluency. The five task characteristics that they looked at were familiarity of the information in the task, whether the task involved a monologue or a dialogue, the degree of structure to the task, the complexity of the task outcome, and the extent to which speakers were required to transform language and content as they spoke. The effects of these characteristics on complexity, accuracy and fluency are summarized in the following table.

Task characteristic	Accuracy	Complexity	Fluency
Familiarity of information	No effect	No effect	Slightly greater
Dialogic versus monologic task	Greater	Slightly greater	Lower
Degree of structure	No effect	No effect	Greater
Complexity of outcome	No effect	Greater	No effect
Transformation	No effect	Planned condition Generates greater complexity	No effect

This research has significant implications for task-based testing. As Skehan (2001: 182) points out:

> If candidate performances are compared after having been elicited through the use of different tasks, the performances themselves may be very difficult to relate to one another. Different candidates, in other words, might be disadvantaged by the particular task that they might have taken as part of their test, and so their performance may not be directly comparable to the other candidates'.

161

Objectives-based criteria

The following checklist was developed to assess a task-based writing program. Here, the criteria are taken directly from the course objectives. Students are assessed on their first and final drafts using the same criteria, and are thus able to see where they have improved and where they have not.

CRITERIA	First draft	Final draft
1. The opening paragraph contains a clear thesis statement.	0 / 1 / 2 / 3 / 4 / 5	0 / 1 / 2 / 3 / 4 / 5
2. The opening paragraph creates interest and/or gives context and/or outlines direction.	0 / 1 / 2 / 3 / 4 / 5	0 / 1 / 2 / 3 / 4 / 5
3. The central argument is supported with appropriate evidence and examples.	0 / 1 / 2 / 3 / 4 / 5	0 / 1 / 2 / 3 / 4 / 5
4. Paragraphs are developed appropriately in terms of cohesion and topicalization.	0 / 1 / 2 / 3 / 4 / 5	0 / 1 / 2 / 3 / 4 / 5
5. Paragraphs are coherent in terms of functional and propositional development.	0 / 1 / 2 / 3 / 4 / 5	0 / 1 / 2 / 3 / 4 / 5
6. The essay is written in an appropriate academic style.	0 / 1 / 2 / 3 / 4 / 5	0 / 1 / 2 / 3 / 4 / 5
7. Citation and biliographical conventions are adhered to.	0 / 1 / 2 / 3 / 4 / 5	0 / 1 / 2 / 3 / 4 / 5
8. The concluding paragraph makes an observation and/or a prediction and/or a recommendation.	0 / 1 / 2 / 3 / 4 / 5	0 / 1 / 2 / 3 / 4 / 5
9. The student is able to paraphrase appropriately.	0 / 1 / 2 / 3 / 4 / 5	0 / 1 / 2 / 3 / 4 / 5
10. The essay is adequately proofed and edited, and is accurate in terms of grammar, spelling and punctuation.	0 / 1 / 2 / 3 / 4 / 5	0 / 1 / 2 / 3 / 4 / 5

Reflect
Consider the following assessment criteria. In what ways do you think that the criteria are problematic?

In the following assessment, you will need to carry out a series of tasks. In some of these tasks you are required to write and speak.

Your writing will be assessed on the following:

Content	The content needs to be **relevant** and **sufficient:** <ul><li>Relevant means the content is meaningful to the topic, and</li><li>Sufficient means that there is enough content (i.e. not too little and not too much).</li></ul>
Organization	Content / Ideas should be presented logically and grouped together or separated in meaningful ways.
Language	<ul><li>You need to make use of a range of **grammatical** and **sentence structures** accurately.</li><li>You need to use a variety of **vocabulary** and **expressions** accurately.</li><li>Your punctuation will be assessed.</li><li>Your spelling needs to be accurate.</li></ul>
Task Requirements	You need to follow the task requirements. For example, a task requirement may limit your writing to 100 words. Therefore read and follow directions carefully.
Leave enough time to proofread your writing.	

Lewkowicz and Nunan (2004)

While it is good that the criteria by which their performance will be judged is made explicit to the learners, the descriptors themselves are problematic. Like most performance-based criteria, the descriptors are relatively vague and imprecise. It is doubtful whether statements such as 'Sufficient means that there is enough content (i.e. not too little and not too much)' are likely to be very useful to learners. Again, what does 'a range of' and 'a variety of' look like in practice?

Conclusion

The purpose of this chapter was to look at aspects of assessment that are pertinent to task-based language teaching. I began with an exploration of key issues in second language assessment, and related these specifically to the context of TBLT. I then looked at practical tools and techniques for assessment including performance scales, production tasks, observation schedules, journals and portfolios. The final part of the chapter examined criteria for assessing learner performance.

I argued that, despite the diverse contexts and situations in which TBLT is carried out, the assessment of learning outcomes should always:

- involve the direct assessment of student performance
- be criterion-referenced
- focus on the attainment of specific objectives rather than trying to assess general proficiency
- be formative in nature.

References

Bailey, K. 1998. *Learning about Language Assessment: Dilemmas, decisions and Directions*. Boston MA: Heinle / Thomson.
Baker, D. 1990. *A Guide to Language Testing*. London: Edward Arnold.
Brindley, G. 1989. *Assessing Achievement in the Learner-Centred Curriculum*. Sydney: National Centre for English Language Teaching and Research.
Brown, J. D. 1989. Improving ESL placement tests using two perspectives. *TESOL Quarterly*, 23, 65–83.
Brown, J. D. and T. Hudson. 2002. *Criterion-Referenced Language Testing*. Cambridge: Cambridge University Press.
Council of Europe. 2001. *Common European Framework of Reference for Language: Learning, teaching, assessment*. Cambridge: Cambridge University Press.
Cram, B. 1995. Self-assessment: from theory to practice. In G. Brindley (ed.) *Language Assessment in Action*. Sydney: National Centre for English Language Teaching and Research.
Education Department. 2001. *Assessment Tasks: Set A*. Hong Kong: Education Department.
Genesee, F. and J. Upshur. 1996. *Classroom-Based Evaluation in Second Language Education*. Cambridge: Cambridge University Press.
Glaser, R. and A. J. Nitko. 1971. Measure in learning and instruction. In R. L. Thorndyke (ed.) *Educational Measurement*. Second edition. Washington DC: American Council on Education.
Gronlund, N. 1981. *Measurement and Evaluation in Education*. New York: Macmillan.

Ingram, D. 1984. *Australian Second Language Proficiency Ratings*. Canberra: Department of Immigration and Ethnic Affairs.

Kemp, J. and D. Toperoff. 1998. Guidelines for portfolio assessment in teaching English. Retrieved 25 September 2002 from http://www.etni.org.il/ministry/portfolio/default.html

Lewkowicz, J. and D. Nunan. 2004. *Task-based Assessment for Learning*. Hong Kong: Hong Kong Education and Manpower Bureau.

Nelson, J. A., K. Chan and A. Swan. 2001. *Longman Express Book 1A*. Hong Kong: Pearson Education North Asia Limited.

Norris, J., J. D. Brown, T. Hudson and J. Yoshioka. 1998. *Designing Second Language Performance Assessments*. Honolulu HI: University of Hawaii.

Nunan, D. 1988. *The Learner-Centred Curriculum*. Cambridge: Cambridge University Press.

Nunan, D. 1996. Learner strategy training in the classroom: an action research study. *TESOL Journal*, 6, 1, 35–41.

Nunan, D. 1999a. *Second Language Teaching and Learning*. Boston: Heinle.

Nunan, D. 1999b. *Go For It: Level 2. Test and games package*. Boston: Heinle.

Nunan, D. 2001. *Expressions: Meaningful English communication. Student book 3*. Boston MA.: Heinle / Thomson.

Nunan, D. and L. Wong. 2003. The e-portfolio as an alternative assessment instrument. Paper presented at the 5th International CULI Conference, Bangkok, Thailand, December 2003.

Ribe, R. and N. Vidal. 1993. *Project Work Step by Step*. 1993. Oxford: Heinemann International.

Richards, J., J. Hull and S. Proctor. 1997. *New Interchange: Student book 1*. Cambridge: Cambridge University Press.

Robinson, P. and S. Ross. 1996. The development of task-based assessment in English for academic purposes programs. *Applied Linguistics*, 17, 4, 455–76.

Savignon, S. and M. Berns (eds). 1984. *Initiatives in Communicative Language Teaching*. Reading Mass.: Addison-Wesley.

Skehan, P. 1998. *A Cognitive Approach to Language Learning*. Oxford: Oxford University Press.

Skehan, P. 2001. Tasks and language performance assessment. In M. Bygate, P. Skehan and M. Swain (eds) 2001. *Researching Pedagogic Tasks: Second language learning, teaching and testing*. London: Longman.

Skehan, P. and P. Foster. 1999. The influence of task structure and processing conditions on narrative retellings. *Language Learning*, 49, 1, 93–120.

Wajnryb, R. 1992. *Classroom Observation Tasks*. Cambridge: Cambridge University Press.

Willis and Willis. 2001. Task-based language learning. In R. Carter and D. Nunan (eds) *The Cambridge Guide to Teaching English for Speakers of Other Languages*. Cambridge: Cambridge University Press.

8 Tasks and teacher development

Introduction and overview

In this final chapter of the book, I want to look at tasks and teacher development. In the first part of the chapter, I will describe a workshop case study where teachers explore the development, application and functioning of tasks in their own professional contexts and situations. The workshop describes ways in which teachers might be encouraged to think more systematically about tasks, and also – as it is a task-based workshop – demonstrates how tasks might be used as the basis for teacher development programs.

In the second half of the chapter, I will examine how to evaluate and create your own tasks. My checklist for evaluating a task draws on input from throughout the book, and should therefore serve as a summary of the salient points introduced in earlier chapters. The checklist can also be used as a tool for creating and developing tasks.

The self-directed teacher

An important trend in language teacher development in recent years has been a move away from the teacher as passive recipient and implementer of other people's syllabuses and methods, towards the idea of the teacher as an active creator of his or her own materials, classroom activities and assessment procedures (Nunan and Lamb 1996). Even in systems which have clearly articulated syllabuses and curriculum guidelines, there is scope for teachers to adapt and modify the syllabuses and materials with which they work. A major aim of this present book, with its points for reflection and analysis, has been to encourage a more self-directed approach on the part of teachers.

Bailey, Curtis and Nunan (2001: 6–7) suggest that there are five reasons why teachers should engage in, and take control of, their own, ongoing professional development:

- to acquire new knowledge and skills
- to cope with, and keep up with, the pace of change

- to increase one's professionalism, status, and even, possibly, income
- to empower oneself through increasing one's knowledge base
- to combat negativity and burnout.

Related to the notion of the self-directed teacher has been a break with the 'method' concept. For many years language teaching has been at the mercy of a number of competing methods. Some of these, such as Suggestopedia, the Silent Way and Community Language Learning, have been rather exotic; others, such as audiolingualism, have been more conservative. (For a comprehensive analysis of a range of the more prominent methods, see Richards and Rodgers 1986.) Despite their diversity, these competing methods have a number of things in common. One of these is the belief that somewhere out there is the 'one best method', that is the method that will work for every conceivable learner in every conceivable context and learning situation. The methods also claim legitimacy in terms of psycholinguistic and psychological learning theory and practice. Thus audiolingualism draws its theoretical rationale from behaviourism, the Total Physical Response was based on selective 'findings' from first language acquisition, and Community Language Learning drew on certain tenets of humanistic psychology.

Richards (1987b) points out that the 'methods' all share something else:

> . . . common to all of them is a set of prescriptions as to what teachers and learners should do in the language classroom. There are prescriptions for the teacher as to what material should be presented, when it should be taught and how, and prescriptions for learners as to what approach they should take towards the teaching materials and classroom activities.

(Richards 1987b: 12)

Reflect
Have you every used one of the methods described above? What was the experience? What are the pros and cons of having a set of 'prescriptions for practice'?

Rather than importing ideas from elsewhere, I suggest that it is preferable to identify what works and what does not work through the direct study of the classroom itself. As it is teachers who are the crucial variable in the teaching situation, it is important that teachers should study what goes on in their own classroom. Self-analysis and evaluation will certainly be characteristics of the self-directed teacher.

In Chapter 1 we saw that the concept of 'task' seemed to be a particularly real one for teachers. Over twenty years ago, in a major study of teachers at work, Swaffar *et al.* (1982) found that teachers tended to plan their work around tasks rather than methods. They concluded that:

> Methodological labels assigned to teaching activities are, in themselves, not informative, because they refer to a pool of classroom practices which are universally used. The differences among major methodologies are to be found in the ordered hierarchy, the priorities assigned to tasks. Not what classroom activity is used, but when and how form the crux of the matter in distinguishing methodological practice.
>
> (Swaffar *et al.* 1982: 31)

In general education, Shavelson and Stern come to the conclusion, that:

> Most teachers are trained to plan instruction by (a) specifying (behavioural) objectives, (b) specifying students' entry behaviour, (c) selecting and sequencing learning behaviours so as to move learners from entry behaviours to objectives and (d) evaluating the outcomes of instruction in order to improve planning. While this prescriptive model of planning may be one of the most consistently taught features of the curriculum of teacher education programs, the model is consistently not used in teachers' planning in schools.
>
> (Shavelson and Stern 1981: 477)

This mismatch between what teachers are taught to do and what they actually do arises, according to Shavelson and Stern, because once inside the classroom the teacher must come up with a constant flow of activities or face behavioural problems. Activities (or tasks as I call them) rather than the prescriptive ends–means model are the major focus of the teacher's planning efforts.

The next section is a case study designed to demonstrate what task-focussed teacher education looks like. Teachers are introduced to the notion of 'task' as a basic tool for program planning and evaluation.

An in-service workshop

This workshop was originally devised as the first in a series on language curriculum design. The concept of 'task' was selected for the initial workshop, as experience has shown that it is the one curriculum element which is most familiar and accessible to classroom teachers. In addition, as Candlin and Murphy (1987) have pointed out, tasks embody a curriculum in miniature. It was therefore felt that a workshop on tasks would provide a 'user-friendly' introduction to wider curriculum issues.

Step 1: Pre-workshop task

Teaches are asked in advance of the workshop to provide a detailed description of a task which works particularly well for them. They are asked to provide information on the target audience for the task, the goal(s), activities, learner roles and groupings.

Step 2: The 'good' language learning task

The first workshop activity is designed to get participants to identify those characteristics which they feel the 'good' language task should possess. To this end, they are asked to rate a series of statements from 0 to 4 according to whether these statements were characteristic of the 'good' task. The statements were taken from a variety of sources (some of which you will recognize from preceding chapters) and are set out below.

Questionnaire on the 'good' learning task

What do you believe?
Circle the appropriate number according to the following scale:
0 – this is not a characteristic of a good task
1 – this characteristic may be present, but is optional
2 – this characteristic is reasonably important
3 – this characteristic is extremely important
4 – this characteristic is essential

Good learning tasks should:

1.	enable learners to manipulate and practise specific features of language	0/1/2/3/4
2.	allow learners to rehearse, in class, communicative skills they will need in the real world	0/1/2/3/4
3.	activate psychological/psycholinguistic processes of learning	0/1/2/3/4
4.	be suitable for mixed ability groups	0/1/2/3/4
5.	involve learners in solving a problem, coming to a conclusion	0/1/2/3/4
6.	be based on authentic or naturalistic source materials	0/1/2/3/4
7.	involve learners in sharing information	0/1/2/3/4
8.	require the use of more than one macroskill	0/1/2/3/4
9.	allow learners to think and talk about language and learning	0/1/2/3/4
10.	promote skills in learning-how-to-learn	0/1/2/3/4
11.	have clear objectives stating what learners will be able to do as a result of taking part in the task	0/1/2/3/4

⤷

12.	utilize the community as a resource	0/1/2/3/4
13.	give learners a choice in what they do and the order in which they do it	0/1/2/3/4
14.	involve learners in risk-taking	0/1/2/3/4
15.	require learners to rehearse, rewrite and polish initial efforts	0/1/2/3/4
16.	enable learners to share in the planning and development of the task	0/1/2/3/4
17.	have built into them a means of evaluating the success or otherwise of the task	0/1/2/3/4

Step 3: Selecting essential characteristics

Having completed the questionnaire on their own, participants then work in pairs to select the five characteristics which they consider to be essential to a good task. This step involves considerable negotiation for those participants who disagree with their partner (and there is usually some disagreement amongst most groups). When disagreements arise, participants are asked to consider why they disagree, to provide evidence for their views, and to identify whether this evidence is based on fact, experience or opinion.

Step 4: Task analysis

Once participants have established their criteria, they are given copies of the tasks sent in by participants prior to the workshop. These are presented in a way that makes it impossible for the authors to be identified. They are asked to rate each task from 0 to 3 according to the extent to which they embody each of the criteria of a good task that the participants themselves have nominated. The scale they are asked to use is as follows:

0 this task does not reflect the criteria at all
1 this task slightly reflects the criteria
2 this task gives the criteria quite a lot of prominence
3 this task gives the criteria a great deal of prominence

This step has to be handled with some care. The principal aim of the exercise is not to criticize the tasks but to encourage participants to evaluate the criteria they have selected against the sorts of tasks they have originally provided. At the end of the workshop, participants very often state that they have given low ratings to their own tasks, and that the exercise has prompted them to review their approach to task selection.

Step 5: Criteria for determining task difficulty

Step 5 is devoted to the issue of task difficulty. The following sets of criteria, from a variety of sources, are provided to participants who want to use them. They are asked to discuss these and come up with their own list of criteria for determining task difficulty.

Factors to be taken into consideration in determining task difficulty

Brindley (1987) considers that learner, task and text factors interact to determine task difficulty:

Easier	More difficult
Learner	
is confident about task	is not confident
is motivated to carry out task	is not motivated
has necessary prior learning experiences	no prior experiences
can learn at pace required	cannot learn at required pace
has necessary language skills	does not have language skills
has relevant cultural knowledge	no relevant cultural knowledge
Task	
low cognitive complexity	cognitively complex
has few steps	has many steps
plenty of context provided	no context
plenty of help available	no help available
does not require grammatical accuracy	grammatical accuracy required
has as much time as necessary	has little time
Text	
is short, not dense (few facts)	is long and dense (many facts)
clear presentation	presentation not clear
plenty of contextual clues	few contextual clues
familiar, everyday content	unfamiliar content

≫→

Brown and Yule (1983): focus on how factors related to the speaker, listener, content, support and purpose will affect task difficulty:

Easier	More difficult
one speaker	many speakers
interesting/involving	boring/non-involving
simple syntax	complex syntax
specific vocabulary	generalized vocabulary
familiar content	unfamiliar content
narratives/instructions	argument/explanation/opinion
temporal sequence	non-temporal sequence
contextual support	no contextual support
visual aids present	visual aids absent
learner involved as a participant	learner as observer

Nunan (1985) sees difficulty as determined by the type of learner response required:

	Comprehension	*Production*	*Interaction*
Easier	Listen/read, no response	Listen/read and repeat/copy	Listen/read, rehearse
	Listen/read, non-verbal response	Listen/read, carry out drill	Listen/read, role play
More difficult	Listen/read, verbal response meaningfully	Listen/read, respond	Listen/read, solve problem/come to conclusion

Anderson and Lynch (1988) see difficulty as determined by information sequence, topic familiarity, explicitness, non-verbal support and item correspondence.

Easier	More difficult
information presented in sequence	information out of sequence
topic is familiar	topic is unfamiliar
graphic/non-verbal support present	graphic support absent

item correspondence: blank – repetition – synonym – compatible – ambiguous – contradictory

Step 6: Applying difficulty criteria

In the final step, participants are given sets of sample tasks and are asked to rank these from the easiest to the most difficult according to the criteria they selected in Step 5.

Reflect
Do your own self-directed mini-workshop. Select a task that works well for you and work through the various steps set out above.

Evaluating tasks

One of the most obvious ways of applying the information presented in the preceding chapters is in task evaluation. This involves adopting a more critical attitude towards the classroom tasks that form the basis of one's teaching program.

In his paper on task design, Candlin (1987) suggests that task evaluation should cover three broad areas. These are 'problematicity', 'implementability' and 'combinability'. 'Problematicity' refers to the extent to which a given task reveals variations in learners' abilities and knowledge, the extent to which it is diagnostic or explanatory, whether it provides monitoring and feedback, and whether it can be used as a basis for future action. 'Implementability' involves a consideration of the resources required, the organizational and management complexity, and the adaptability of the task. Finally 'combinability' requires us to consider the extent to which the task can be sequenced and integrated with other tasks.

The following checklist contains a set of questions for evaluating tasks. These reflect the various issues and concepts already covered in the preceding chapters. The list of questions can be used in a variety of ways. You will not necessarily need or want to answer all the questions in task evaluation. I would suggest that at particular times (when, for example, you are trying out a new task for the first time, or using a task which is familiar to you but not to your students) you record the lesson in which the task is introduced on audio- or videotape and use this to aid your reflection as you evaluate the task. An alternative would be to invite a colleague to observe your class and do the evaluation with you.

Checklist for evaluating tasks

Goals and rationale
– To what extent is the goal or goals of the task obvious a) to you, b) to your students?
– Is the task appropriate to the learners' proficiency level?
– To what extent does the task reflect a real-world or pedagogic rationale? Is this appropriate?
– Does the task encourage learners to apply classroom learning to the real world?
– What beliefs about the nature of language and learning are inherent in the task?
– Is the task likely to be interesting and motivating to the students?

Input
– What form does the input take?
– Is it authentic?
– If not, is it appropriate to the goal(s) of the task?

Procedures
– Are the procedures appropriate to the goal(s) of the task?
– If not, can they be modified to make them more appropriate?
– Is the task designed to stimulate students to use bottom–up or top–down processing skills?
– Is there an information gap or problem which might prompt a negotiation of meaning?
– Are the procedures appropriate to the input data?
– Are the procedures designed in a way which will allow learners to communicate and cooperate in groups?
– Is there a learning strategies dimension, and is this made explicit to the learners?
– Is there a focus on form aspect and, if so, how is this realized?

Roles and settings
– What learner and teacher roles are inherent in the task?
– Are they appropriate?
– What levels of complexity are there in the classroom organization implicit in the task?
– Is the setting confined to the classroom?

Implementation
– Does the task actually engage the learners' interest?
– Do the procedures prompt genuine communicative interaction among students?
– To what extent are learners encouraged to negotiate meaning?

− Does anything unexpected occur as the task is being carried out?
− What type of language is actually stimulated by the task?
− Is this different from what might have been predicted?

Grading
− Is the task at the appropriate level of difficulty for the students?
− If not, is there any way in which the task might be modified in order to make it either easier or more challenging?
− Is the task structured so that it can be undertaken at different levels of difficulty?

Integration
− What are the principles upon which tasks are sequenced?
− Do tasks exhibit the 'task continuity' principle?
− Are a range of macroskills integrated into the sequence of tasks?
− If not, can you think of ways in which they might be integrated?
− At the level of the unit or lesson, are communicative tasks integrated with other activities and exercises designed to provide learners with mastery of the linguistic system?
− If not, are there ways in which such activities might be introduced?
− Do tasks incorporate exercises in learning-how-to-learn?
− If not, are there ways in which such exercises might be introduced?

Assessment and evaluation
− What means exist for the teacher to determine how successfully the learners have performed?
− Does the task have built into it some means whereby learners might judge how well they have performed?
− Is the task realistic in terms of the resources and teacher-expertise it demands?

Creating tasks

In addition to its use as a tool for evaluating tasks that may have been created by others, the checklist can also be used to guide you in creating and critiquing your own tasks.

As we have already seen, the starting point for task design should be the goals and objectives which are set out in the syllabus or curriculum guidelines that underpin your teaching program. You may need to augment or modify these if they are not written in a form which can be directly translated into communicative tasks. Objectives may, for instance, be set out as checklists of grammatical items, such as the following:

At the end of the course learners will be able to use the present con-tinuous tense to describe actions in progress.

Most syllabuses and curriculum guidelines will provide some sort of rationale. This may be a broad statement of intent, such as:

The course should develop reading and writing skills for tertiary study.

or

The focus will be on the survival skills needed by learners in the target culture.

Even these very general statements provide a point of departure for task design.

The next step is selecting or creating input for learners to work with. In the preceding chapters, we have seen that the use of authentic input is a central characteristic of task-based language teaching. You will need to consider the extent to which it is possible for you to use authentic data. Your decision will depend on such factors as the attitude of your learn-ers and the availability of resources. Many low-level learners are trau-matized when first exposed to authentic samples of language, and have to be taught that it is not necessary to understand every word for com-munication to be successful. Teachers working in a foreign language context will be faced with greater difficulty in obtaining authentic samples of input than second language teachers, particularly in obtain-ing aural input data, although the media and the Internet greatly facili-tate matters these days.

Where possible, it is desirable to build up a 'bank' of data. These can be classified and filed under topics or themes, and provide a ready-made resource to be drawn on when designing tasks. As indicated earlier, one should work from the data to the teaching/learning objectives, rather than the other way round. In other words, it is better to derive commu-nicative activities and other exercises, such as grammatical manipulation exercises, from the input, rather than, say, deciding to teach a particular item, and then creating a text to exemplify the target feature or item.

When designing activities, you need to decide whether you want learn-ers to rehearse in class tasks which they will, potentially at least, want to carry out in the real world. If the tasks have a pedagogic rationale, you need to be clear what this is. You also need to consider the role that both you and the learners will adopt in carrying out the task and assess whether these roles are appropriate to the given group. Settings and learner configurations also need to be considered. Getting learners in and out of groups of different sizes quickly and efficiently so that time on the task is maximized is an important classroom management skill.

When monitoring the task, you will want to keep a close check on the actual language which is generated, particularly if it is a focused task. This will often differ from what had been predicted. It is a good idea to record teacher-fronted and small group interactions from time to time and use these to review and evaluate the task.

Conclusion

In this final chapter, I have broadened the focus to show how a task-based approach can be used in teacher development. Tasks can also be used as a point of departure for small-scale classroom research projects by teachers themselves. Such projects should lead teachers to see the relevance of the theory for the practical concerns of the classroom.

Postscript

In language teaching, as in general education, there has been a move away from a top–down approach to the planning, implementation and evaluation of teaching programs. The top-down approach is characterized by curriculum plans, syllabus outlines and methodological procedures which are designed by 'experts' and delivered as a package to the classroom practitioner. In-service and professional development programs are principally designed to train teachers how to use these externally developed syllabuses, materials and methods. As I mentioned briefly earlier in this chapter, in language teaching, the top–down approach resulted in a spate of methods developed during the 1960s and early 1970s. Alongside audiolingualism and cognitive code learning, there were the more exotic methods such as Total Physical Response (Asher 1977), Community Language Learning (Curran 1976), Suggestopedia (the most accessible introduction to the principles of Suggestopedia is Ostrander and Schroeder 1981) and, more recently, the 'Natural' Approach (Krashen and Terrell 1983). These methods are described and criticized in Richards and Rodgers (1986). (A table summarizing these various approaches and derived from Richards and Rodgers is included as Appendix A.) Most of these methods have one thing in common: they assume that there is one best way of learning a second or foreign language, and they provide a set of principles and procedures, which, it is believed, if followed properly by the classroom practitioner, will result in learning.

With the recent break from the 'method' concept has come the development of more bottom–up approaches to language teaching. The curriculum is being rediscovered, not as a set of prescriptive edicts, but as the documentation and systematization of classroom practice (Nunan 1988a). Curriculum designers are becoming concerned with identifying principles of effective teaching from within the classroom itself. This is reflected in the ongoing interest in classroom-oriented research (see, for example, Bailey 1999).

Another theme which has been reiterated in various guises in recent years is the need in pre- and in-service teacher education programs for a balance between theory and practice. It is also important for participants to appreciate the complementary nature of theory and practice. This is unlikely to be achieved in teacher education programs in which the theoretical and practical components are kept apart. Bottom-up and classroom-oriented approaches to curriculum development, on the other hand, are particularly amenable to achieving an appropriate balance between theory and practice.

A major trend in language teaching in recent years has been the adoption of learner-centred approaches to curriculum development. Learner-centred approaches are characterized by the involvement of the learner, and the utilization of information about the learner in all aspects of the curriculum process (Nunan 1988a: 6).

Brundage and MacKeracher (1980) and Knowles (1983) argue for a client-centred approach to adult learning on the grounds that adults value their own experience as a resource for further learning, and that they learn best when they have a personal investment in the program and when the content is personally relevant.

Given the trends and issues which I have just referred to, I would like to propose the following principles for teacher development programs, particularly post-experience or in-service programmes. Here, teachers are looking for guidance in solving problems which confront them in the classroom. Therefore, there must be explicit links between the content of professional development programs and the classroom.

1. Content and methodology should be perceived as being personally relevant;
2. theory should be derived from practice;
3. the approach should be bottom–up rather than top–down;
4. teachers should be involved in the structuring of the professional development programme;
5. content should, as far as possible, be derived from the teachers themselves;
6. desirable practices should be modelled in the professional development program;

and last but not least, given the focus of this book, because they are particularly salient for teachers and also because they provide a convenient point of entry into other areas of curriculum planning, implementation and evaluation:

7. tasks should be given a prominent place in pre- and in-service professional development programs designed to introduce participants to principles of curriculum design and development.

One of the most effective ways of incorporating these principles into teacher development programs is to use input from teachers themselves. We have seen one way in which this might work, although there are many other variants. For example, one might give all workshop participants some input several weeks in advance of the workshop and ask them to a) create a task based on the input; b) get their students to undertake the task; c) record them as they do so. The workshop would then consist of participants describing their tasks along the lines already suggested (i.e. in terms of goals, input, activities, learner and teacher roles and evaluation). Following this, they could look at similarities and differences and make suggestions as to how and why these came about. The coordinator could then bring the workshop to a conclusion with a summary of the theory and principles underlying the discussions.

Extending the principle of teacher input forming the basis of professional development workshops, it is usually possible to get teachers to identify some issue, problem or question which they would like to follow up. Teachers would set up a small-scale investigation in their classroom and report back to the workshop group at a later date. In this way, teachers can be encouraged to adopt an action research orientation to their work. Such an orientation allows theory to be integrated with practice.

References

Anderson, A., and T. Lynch. 1988. *Listening*. Oxford: Oxford University Press.

Asher, J. 1977. *Learning Another Language Through Actions: the complete teacher's guide book*. Los Gatos Calif.: Sky Oaks Productions.

Bailey, K. 1999. What have we learned from 25 years of classroom research? Plenary presentation, International TESOL Convention, New York, March 1999.

Bailey, K., A. Curtis and D. Nunan. 2001. *Pursuing Professional Development: the self as source*. Boston MA: Heinle.

Brindley, G. 1987. Factors affecting task difficulty. In D. Nunan (ed.) *Guidelines for the Development of Curriculum Resources for the Adult Migrant Education Program*. Adelaide: National Curriculum Resource Centre.

Brown, G. and G. Yule. 1983. *Teaching the Spoken Language*. Cambridge: Cambridge University Press.

Brundage, D. H. and D. MacKeracher 1980. *Adult Learning Principles and Their Application to Program Planning*. Ontario: Ontario Institute for Studies in Education.

Candlin, C. 1987. *Language Learning Tasks*. Englewood Cliffs, N.J.: Prentice-Hall International.

Chaudron, C. 1988. *Second Language Classrooms: Research on teaching and learning*. Cambridge: Cambridge University Press.

Curran, C. 1976. *Counselling-Learning in Second Languages*. Apple River Ill.: Apple River Press.

Knowles, M. 1983. *The Adult Learner: a neglected species*. Houston: Gulf Publishing Company.

Krashen, S. and T. Terrell. 1983. *The Natural Approach*. Oxford: Pergamon Press.

Nunan, D. 1985. *Language Teaching Course Design: Trends and issues*. Adelaide: National Curriculum Resource Centre.

Nunan, D. 1988a. *The Learner-Centred Curriculum*. Cambridge: Cambridge University Press.

Nunan, D. 1988b. *Syllabus Design*. Oxford: Oxford University Press.

Nunan, D. and C. Lamb. 1996. *The Self-Directed Teacher*. Cambridge: Cambridge University Press.

Ostrander, S. and L. Schroeder. 1981. *Superlearning*. London: Sphere Books.

Ramani, E. 1987. Theorizing from the classroom. *English Language Teaching Journal*, 41, 1, 3–11.

Richards, J. 1987. Beyond methods: alternative approaches to instructional design in language teaching. *Prospect*, 3, 1, 11–30.

Richards, J. and T. Rodgers. 1986. *Approaches and Methods in Language Teaching*. Cambridge: Cambridge University Press.

Seliger, H. and M. Long. 1983. *Classroom-Oriented Research*. Rowley Mass.: Newbury House.

Shavelson, R. J. and P. Stern. 1981. Research on teachers' pedagogical thoughts, judgements, decisions and behaviour. *Review of Educational Research*, 51, 4.

Swaffar, J., K. Arens and M. Morgan. 1982. Teacher classroom practices: redefining method as task hierarchy. *Modern Language Journal*, 66, 1.

van Lier, L. 1988. *The Classroom and the Language Learner: Ethnography and second-language classroom research*. London: Longman.

Appendix A   Approaches and methods – an overview

Theory of language	Theory of learning	Objectives	Syllabus
Oral Situational Language Teaching			
Language is a set of structures, related to situations.	Memorization and habit formation.	To teach a practical command of the four basic skills. Automatic, accurate control of basic sentence patterns. Oral before written mastery.	A list of structures and vocabulary graded according to grammatical difficulty.
Audiolingual			
Language is a system of rule-governed structures hierarchically arranged.	Habit formation; skills are learned more effectively if oral precedes written; analogy not analysis.	Control of the structures of sound, form and order mastery over symbols of the language; goal is native-speaker mastery.	Graded syllabus of phonology, morphology and syntax. Contrastive analysis.
Communicative			
Language is a system for the expression of meaning; primary function–interaction and communication.	Activities involving real communication; carrying out meaningful tasks and using language which is meaningful to the learner to promote learning.	Objectives will reflect the needs of the learner; they will include functional skills as well as linguistic objectives.	Will include some/all of the following: structures, functions, notions, themes, tasks. Ordering will be guided by learner needs.
Total Physical Response			
Basically a structuralist, grammar-based view of language.	L2 learning is the same as L1 learning; comprehension before production is 'imprinted' through carrying out commands (right brain	To teach oral proficiency to produce learners who can communicate uninhibitedly and intelligibly with native speakers.	Sentence-based syllabus with grammatical and lexical criteria being primary, but focus on meaning not form.

functioning); reduction of
stress.

	View of language	Theory of learning	Objectives	Syllabus
The Silent Way	Each language is composed of elements that give it a unique rhythm and spirit. Functional vocabulary and core structure are a key to the spirit of the language.	Processes of learning a second language are fundamentally different from L1 learning. L2 learning is an intellectual, cognitive process. Surrender to the music of the language, silent awareness then active trial.	Near-native fluency, correct pronunciation, basic practical knowledge of the grammar of the L2. Learner learns how to learn a language.	Basically structural lessons planned around grammatical items and related vocabulary. Items are introduced according to their grammatical complexity.
Community Language Learning	Language is more than a system for communication. It involves the whole person, culture, educational, developmental, communicative processes.	Learning involves the whole person. It is a social process of growth from childlike dependence to self-direction and independence.	No specific objectives. Near-native mastery is the goal.	No set syllabus. Course progression is topic-based; learners provide the topics. Syllabus emerges from learners' intention and the teacher's reformulations.
The Natural Approach	The essence of language is meaning. Vocabulary not grammar is the heart of language.	There are two ways of L2 language development: 'acquisition' – a natural subconscious process, and 'learning' – a conscious process. Learning cannot lead to acquisition.	Designed to give beginners and intermediate learners basic (oral/written) personal and academic communicative skills.	Based on a selection of communicative activities and topics derived from learner needs.

Theory of language	Theory of learning	Syllabus	Objectives
Suggestopedia Rather conventional, although memorization of whole meaningful texts is recommended.	Learning occurs through suggestion, when learners are in a deeply relaxed state. Baroque music is used to induce this state.	Ten-unit courses consisting of 1,200-word dialogues graded by vocabulary and grammar	To deliver advanced conversational competence quickly. Learners are required to master prodigious lists of vocabulary pairs, although the goal is understanding not memorization.

Activity types	Learner roles	Teacher roles	Roles of materials
Oral Situational Language Teaching Repetition, substitution drills; avoid translation and grammatical explanation; learners should never be allowed to make a mistake.	To listen and repeat, respond to questions and commands; learner has no control over content; later allowed to initiate statements and ask questions.	Acts as a model in presenting structures; orchestrates drill practice; corrects errors, tests progress.	Relies on textbook and visual aids; textbook contains tightly organized, structurally graded lessons.
Audiolingual Dialogues and drills, repetition and memorization, pattern practice.	Organisms that can be directed by skilled training techniques to produce correct responses.	Teacher-dominated; central and active teacher provides modes, controls direction and pace.	Primarily teacher oriented. Tapes, visuals and language laboratory often used.
Communicative Engage learners in communication, involving	Learner as negotiator and interactor who gives as well	Facilitator of the communication process;	Primary role of promoting communicative language

	Learner roles	Teacher roles	Materials
processes such as information sharing, negotiation of meaning and interaction.	as takes.	needs analyst counsellor; process manager.	use; task-based materials; authentic.
Total Physical Response Imperative drills to elicit physical actions.	Listener and performer; little influence over the content of learning.	Active and direct role as 'the director of a stage play' with students as actors.	No basic text; materials and media have an important role later. Initially voice, action and gestures are sufficient.
The Silent Way Learner responses to commands, questions and visual cues. Activities encourage and shape oral responses without grammatical explanation or modelling by teacher.	Learning is a process of personal growth. Learners are responsible for their own learning and must develop independence, autonomy and responsibility.	Teachers must a) teach, b) test and c) get out of the way; remain impassive. Resist temptation to model, remodel, assist, direct exhort.	Unique materials: coloured rods, colour-coded pronunciation and vocabulary charts.
Community Language Learning Combination of innovative and conventional. Translation, group work, recording, transcription, reflection and observation, listening, free conversation.	Learners are members of a community. Learning is not viewed as an individual accomplishment, but something that is achieved collaboratively.	Counselling/parental analogy. Teacher provides a safe environment in which students can learn and grow.	No textbook, which would inhibit growth. Materials are developed as course progresses.

Activity types	Learner roles	Teacher roles	Roles of materials
The Natural Approach Activities allowing comprehensible input about things in the here-and-now. Focus on meaning not form.	Should not try and learn language in the usual sense, but should try and lose themselves in activities involving meaningful communication.	The teacher is the primary source of comprehensible input. Must create positive low-anxiety climate. Must choose and orchestrate a rich mixture of classroom activities.	Materials come from realia rather then textbooks. Primary aim is to promote comprehension and communication.
Suggestopedia Initiatives, question and answer, role play, listening exercises under deep relaxation.	Must maintain a passive state and allow the materials to work on them (rather than *vice versa*).	To create situations in which the learner is most suggestible, and present material in a way most likely to encourage positive reception and retention. Must exude authority and confidence.	Consists of texts, tapes, classroom fixtures and music. Texts should have force, literary quality and interesting characters.

Appendix B A unit of work based on the six-step procedure presented in Chapter 2

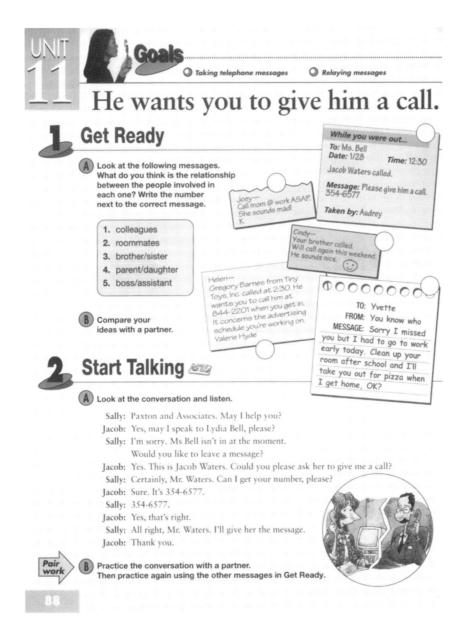

UNIT 11

Goals ....
○ Taking telephone messages   ○ Relaying messages

He wants you to give him a call.

1 Get Ready

A Look at the following messages. What do you think is the relationship between the people involved in each one? Write the number next to the correct message.

1. colleagues
2. roommates
3. brother/sister
4. parent/daughter
5. boss/assistant

B Compare your ideas with a partner.

While you were out...
To: Ms. Bell
Date: 1/28   Time: 12:30
Jacob Waters called.
Message: Please give him a call.
354-6577
Taken by: Audrey

Joey—
Call mom @ work ASAP.
She sounds mad!
K

Cindy—
Your brother called.
Will call again this weekend.
He sounds nice. ☺

Helen—
Gregory Barnes from Tiny Toys, Inc. called at 2:30. He wants you to call him at 844-2201 when you get in. It concerns the advertising schedule you're working on.
Valerie Hyde

TO: Yvette
FROM: You know who
MESSAGE: Sorry I missed you but I had to go to work early today. Clean up your room after school and I'll take you out for pizza when I get home, OK?

2 Start Talking

A Look at the conversation and listen.

Sally: Paxton and Associates. May I help you?
Jacob: Yes, may I speak to Lydia Bell, please?
Sally: I'm sorry. Ms Bell isn't in at the moment.
       Would you like to leave a message?
Jacob: Yes. This is Jacob Waters. Could you please ask her to give me a call?
Sally: Certainly, Mr. Waters. Can I get your number, please?
Jacob: Sure. It's 354-6577.
Sally: 354-6577.
Jacob: Yes, that's right.
Sally: All right, Mr. Waters. I'll give her the message.
Jacob: Thank you.

Pair work
B Practice the conversation with a partner.
Then practice again using the other messages in Get Ready.

88

3 Listen In

A You will hear three people taking messages. Listen and correct the mistakes in the messages below.

❶
TO: Mr. Vasquez
FROM: Mr. Parker
TEL: 902-3500
Please call this afternoon.

❷
Brenda—
Connie called. Meeting at Cultural Center changed to 7:30.
—Liz

❸
Marjorie—
Jeremy Bryant called. Please call between 4 and 6. Says you have his number.
—Stephen

B What do you think is the relationship between the caller and the person he/she is trying to call? Listen again and check ( ) all you think could be correct.

	boss	client	co-worker	friend	brother/sister
1.					
2.					
3.					

C Compare your ideas with a partner.

Try this

In Conversation 2, how did Liz signal that she's ready to take the message? Can you remember?

4 Say It Right

A The letters of the alphabet can be put into seven categories by the vowel sound they contain. Work with a partner and finish filling in the chart with the other letters.

/eɪ/	/i/	/ɛ/	/aɪ/	/ou/	/u/	/ɑ/
A	B	F	I	O	Q	R

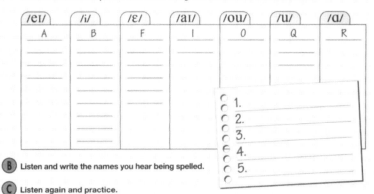

1.
2.
3.
4.
5.

B Listen and write the names you hear being spelled.

C Listen again and practice.

He wants you to give him a call.   89

188

5 Focus In

A Look at the chart.

ask/want/tell

Can I take a message? Would you like to leave a message?	Could you please **ask her to** call Mr. Neal? Can you please **tell her (that)** I phoned? Could you **tell her to** give me a call?
Hi, Gary. Any messages for me?	Yes, Mr. Neal called. He **wants you to** give him a call.

B Match the statements with the responses.

1. I need to speak to Jim.
2. Jacob Walters called while you were out.
3. Susie called while you were out.
4. Grace was late for work again this morning.
5. Sorry, he's on another line at the moment.

_____ Tell her to get a better alarm clock.
_____ Did you ask her to call back?
_____ Could you ask him to call me back?
_____ Did you tell him I'd be back by two?
_____ OK. I'll ask him to call you.

C Write answers to the question below using the words shown.

Ms. Jones is out at the moment. Can I take a message?

1. (tell/David called) _____
2. (ask/call me back) _____
3. (tell/call/Boston headquarters) _____
4. (ask/fax this month's figures) _____

6 Talk Some More

> When reporting a request, instead of *He wants you to...* you can say *He asked if you would...*

A Fill in the missing information.

Ms. Bell: Hi, Audrey. Any messages for me?
Audrey: Yes, Ms. Bell. Jacob Walters _____. He _____ you to give him a call.
Ms. Bell: Did you _____ his number?
Audrey: Yes, I wrote it down. Here it is.
Ms. Bell: Great. What time did he _____?
Audrey: Around 12:30.
Ms. Bell: OK. Thanks.
Audrey: You're welcome.

B Check your answers.

Pair work **C** Practice the conversation with a partner.
Then practice again using the messages in Listen In.

90 Unit 11

189

Appendix B

Student B: Use page 92

Work In Pairs (Student A)

Ⓐ Look at the messages. Underline the parts of each message you think are most important.

Your sister Pat called at 1. Maybe coming to visit next week. Will call tonight, or call her at work 620-4487 ext. 376.

Benny called at 2:15. Has important news. Call him back before 8:00. 492-0579

Dr. Olson's office called at 11:30. Reconfirming your appointment at 5 on June 3.

Francine Miller from Shetland Pharmaceuticals. Says there is a problem w/ their order and wants to talk to you personally. Please fax a copy of their purchase order to (532) 447-0173. Will call back after receiving P.O.

Ⓑ Imagine you took the messages above. Pass them on to your partner. Remember to use complete sentences.

Oh, Scott, Barbie called this afternoon. She wants you to give her a call. She says she can't wait to see you at school tomorrow.

Ⓒ Your partner has taken some messages for you. Get the messages and note the important information. Then check with your partner.

1. _____
2. _____
3. _____
4. _____

Try this

Change the details in one of your messages (name, time, phone number, etc.). Pass on the message to your partner. Did your partner note the information correctly?

_____
_____
_____

He wants you to give him a call. **91**

190

Work In Pairs   (Student B)

Student A: Use page 91

(A) Look at the messages. Underline the parts of each message you think are most important.

Lester from Finance Dept. called this morning. Wanted to congratulate you on your promotion. Says he'll see you at Friday office meeting.

Debra wants you to call her at 4. Just wants to chat. She's at Ruth's. (338-9275)

Danny stopped by during lunch. Wanted to surprise you. Says sorry he missed you. Call him if you have time @ 440-2964.

Mr. Worthington called from the Westport Hotel at 5:30. Will be about 15 min. late. Please wait in lobby. Can reach him by cell phone at 102-887-2633

(B) Your partner has taken some messages for you. Get the messages and note the important information. Then check with your partner.

Oh, Scott, Barbie called this afternoon. She wants you to give her a call. She says she can't wait to see you at school tomorrow.

1.

2.

3.

4.

(C) Imagine you took the messages in 'A' above. Pass them on to your partner. Remember to use complete sentences.

Try this

Change the details in one of your messages (name, time, phone number, etc.). Pass on the message to your partner. Did your partner note the information correctly?

Appendix B

8 Express Yourself

Pair work

(A) Call your partner and leave messages for three people in your class. Also note the messages your partner gives you on a piece of paper.

Mr. Dithers? I'm sorry. He's not available right now. Can I take a message?

(B) Pass on the three messages to the correct people in your class. Also note any messages you receive from other people.

(C) Check the messages you received with the original senders. Were the messages correct?

9 *Think About It*

In many cultures, it's important to be polite on the phone. This is especially true if you have to ask someone to wait. Here are some examples:

- *Just a moment, please. I'll check for you.*
- *Can you hold on a second, please? I'll write this down.*
- *Hold the line, please. I'll transfer your call.*

• *How about in your culture? What polite expressions do you have for talking on the phone?*

10 Write About It

(A) Look at the note.

> Lisa,
> I'll be back around 6:00 or so, but I'm expecting an important phone call before then. If you get a call from Ms. Peterson, could you ask her to call me back after 6:30? Or if she leaves her phone number, could you tell her that I'll call her back as soon as I get home?
> Thanks a lot!
> Marty

(B) Write a note asking a friend to do something for you.

He wants you to give him a call.   93

Read On   The Homing Instinct

• *Strategy: Reading actively*

How could you send a message long-distance, without a phone, radio or email?

Read these statements. Then read the article and check (✓) *True* or *False*.   *True*   *False*

1. Years ago, empires used pigeons to send messages over very short distances.   ☐   ☐

2. Pigeons played an important role in the postal system in ancient China.   ☐   ☐

3. The Reuters news agency originally used pigeons as a way to send messages.   ☐   ☐

4. Pigeons brought messages from Napoleon directly to Nathan Rothschild.   ☐   ☐

5. French pigeons were sent to Britain in special boxes during World War II.   ☐   ☐

6. Pigeon-racing is a popular hobby for many people today.   ☐   ☐

For thousands of years, humans have used carrier pigeons as a means of communicating with other people. While horse-riders and caravans might take weeks to carry a message from one end of an empire to another, specially-trained pigeons could pass the message over a long distance in a much shorter time. Pigeon networks were used in the vast empires of Egypt, Rome and Carthage; China even organized an extensive postal system based upon the use of pigeons.

Carrier pigeons, also known as 'messenger' pigeons or 'racing' pigeons, have also helped to create great fortunes as well as empires. The Reuters news agency, for example, was founded as a line of pigeon posts in the nineteenth century. In 1815, businessman Nathan Rothschild used his pigeons to keep him informed of developments at the Battle of Waterloo. He used his information about Napoleon's defeat to buy large numbers of government bonds before their values increased. Rothschild's pigeons thus helped him to become a very rich man.

Pigeons have also long been used to carry messages during wartime. Both sides in Europe during World War II used pigeons to send secret messages. The British parachuted pigeons in special boxes down onto French fields. In the box were questions for French farmers to answer about German movements in the area. If the box was found, the finder was supposed to attach a message to the pigeon and let it fly home. One pigeon was even awarded the Dickens Medal, a reward for bravery, by the Mayor of London!

Now, people all over the world breed and race homing pigeons as a hobby. The pigeon today is still valued for its speed, reliability, endurance and beauty, just as it was thousands of years ago.

Talk About It

○ Do you have a pet? Describe it. Do you think it's intelligent?

○ What other types of animals have helped humans in history? How?

○ How might you send a secret message to someone in this room?

Appendix B

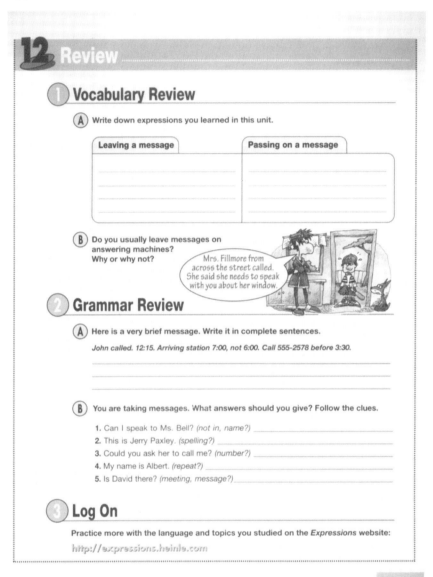

Source: Nunan, D. 2001. *Expressions: Student book 3*. Boston MA: Heinle / Thomson.
Pages 88–95.

Appendix C A unit of work based on the task/exercise typology in Chapter 5

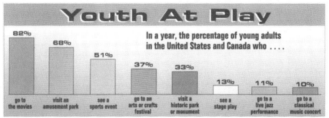

1 SNAPSHOT

Youth At Play

In a year, the percentage of young adults in the United States and Canada who . . . .

82% go to the movies
68% visit an amusement park
51% see a sports event
37% go to an arts or crafts festival
33% visit a historic park or monument
13% see a stage play
11% go to a live jazz performance
10% go to a classical music concert

Source: National Endowment for the Arts

Talk about these questions.

Which of these activities have you done in the past year?
Which of these activities would you like to do?
What other activities do you like to do?

2 CONVERSATION Talking about plans

A Listen and practice.

Tony: Say, Anna, what are you doing tonight?
Would you like to go out?
Anna: Oh, sorry, I can't. I'm going to work
late tonight. I have to finish this report.
Tony: Well, how about tomorrow night?
Are you doing anything then?
Anna: No, I'm not. What are you planning
to do?
Tony: I'm going to see a musical. Would you
like to come?
Anna: Sure, I'd love to! But let *me* pay for the
tickets this time. It's my turn.
Tony: All right! Thanks!

CLASS AUDIO ONLY

B Listen to the rest of the conversation.

1. What musical are they going to see?
2. What are they doing before the musical?
3. Where are they going to meet?
4. What time are they meeting?

92

Appendix C

I'm going to see a musical.

3 GRAMMAR FOCUS

Future with present continuous and be going to

With present continuous	With be going to + verb	Time expressions
What **are** you **doing** tonight?	What **is** she **going to do** tonight?	tonight
I'm going to a movie.	She**'s going to work** late.	tomorrow
Are you **doing** anything tomorrow night?	**Are** they **going to see** a musical tomorrow night?	on Friday
No, I'm not.	Yes, they are.	this weekend
		next week

A Complete the invitations in column A with the present continuous used as future. Complete the responses in column B with *be going to*.

A

1. What .... you .... (do) tomorrow? Would you like to go out?

2. .... you .... (do) anything on Saturday night? Do you want to see a movie?

3. We .... (have) friends over for a barbecue on Sunday. Would you and your parents like to come?

B

a. Well, my father .... (visit) my brother at college. But my mother and I .... (be) home. We'd love to come!

b. Sorry, I can't. I .... (work) overtime. How about Saturday?

c. Can we go to a late show? I .... (stay) at the office till 7:00. After that I .... (go) to the gym.

B Match the invitations in column A with the responses in column B. Then practice with a partner.

4 WORD POWER Leisure activities

Leisure activities

A Complete the word map with activities from the list. Then add two more words to each category.

art show   craft fair
barbecue   hockey game
baseball game picnic
beach party   play
car show   rock concert
comedy act   tennis tournament

Exhibitions

Friendly gatherings

B *Pair work* Are you going to do any of the activities on the chart? When are you doing them? Talk with a partner.

A: I'm going to see a rock concert.
B: Really? When?
A: On Friday.
B: . . .

Spectator sports

Live performances

93

196

Unit 15

5 ROLE PLAY   An invitation

Student A: Choose an activity from Exercise 4 and invite a partner to go
with you. Be ready to say where and when the activity is.

A: Say, are you doing anything on . . . ?
Would you like to . . . ?

Student B: Your partner invites you out. Either accept the invitation and ask
for more information, or say you can't go and give an excuse.

Accept
B: That sounds interesting.
Where is it?

Refuse
B: Oh, I'm sorry, but I can't go.
I'm . . . .

Change roles and try the role play again.

6 CONVERSATION   Telephone messages

Listen and practice.

Secretary: Good morning, Parker Industries.
Mr. Kale: Hello. May I speak to Ms. Graham, please?
Secretary: I'm sorry. She's not in. Can I
take a message?
Mr. Kale: Yes, please. This is Mr. Kale.
Secretary: Is that G-A-L-E?
Mr. Kale: No, it's K-A-L-E.
Secretary: All right.
Mr. Kale: Please tell her our meeting
is on Friday at 2:30.
Secretary: Friday at 2:30.
Mr. Kale: And would you ask her
to call me this afternoon?
My number is 356-4031.
Secretary: 356-4031. Yes, Mr. Kale.
I'll give Ms. Graham
the message.
Mr. Kale: Thank you.
Good-bye.
Secretary: Good-bye.

**What are you
going to do?**

Find out what your
classmates are doing
over the weekend.
Turn to page
IC-20.

To: *Ms. Graham*
Date: *August 10*   Time: _____

WHILE YOU WERE OUT
From: *Mr. Kale*
of: _____
Phone: *356-4031*   ext: _____
Message:
The meeting is on Friday at 2:30.
Please call him this afternoon.
Taken by: _____

94

7 GRAMMAR FOCUS

Tell *and* ask

Statement	Messages with a statement
The meeting is on Friday.	**Please tell Ann (that)** the meeting is on Friday.
	Would you tell her (that) . . . ?
	Could you tell her (that) . . . ?
Request	Messages with a request
Call me this afternoon.	**Please ask him to** call me this afternoon.
	Would you ask him to . . . ?
	Could you tell him to . . . ?

Look at the message slips. Ask someone to pass on these messages.
Use the words in parentheses. Then compare with a partner.

1.
> Kim -
> The movie is at
> 7:00 tonight.

(could) Could you tell Kim the movie is at 7:00?

2.
> Mike -
> Pick me up at home
> around 4:00.

(would)

3.
> Maria -
> The concert on Saturday
> is canceled.

(please)

4.
> Jim -
> Bring the tickets for the
> hockey game tonight.

(could)

5.
> Ann -
> The museum opens at
> 10:00 tomorrow morning.

(would)

6.
> Alex -
> Meet us in front of the
> cafeteria at 12:15.

(please)

8 WRITING

Pair work You want to give messages to people in your class. Write a
request to your partner. Ask him or her to give the messages for you.

> Dear Su Hee,
> I'm not going to be in class tomorrow. Would you please ask Ms. King to save any
> handouts for me? Also, could you tell Steve that I can't meet him for dinner after class?
> Thanks,
> Juan

Unit 15

9 *PRONUNCIATION* Reduced forms of could you *and* would you

A Listen and practice. Notice how **could you** and **would you** are reduced in conversation.

/cudʒə/
Could you tell Matt the meeting is at 5:00?

/wudʒə/
Would you ask him to pick me up at 4:30?

B Practice these questions with reduced forms.

Could you ask her to return my dictionary?
Would you tell him there's a picnic tomorrow?

10 *LISTENING* Take a message

 Listen to telephone calls to Mr. Kim and Ms. Carson, and write down the messages.

1.
> To: *Mr.*
> Date: _____ Time: ____
> **WHILE YOU WERE OUT**
> From: _____
> of: *City*
> Phone: _____ ext: ____
> Message: _____
> _Call Mrs._
> _____
> Taken by: _____

2.
> To: *Wendy*
> Date: _____ Time: ____
> **WHILE YOU WERE OUT**
> From: _____
> of: *National*
> Phone: _____ ext: ____
> Message: _____
> _____
> Taken by: _____

11 *ROLE PLAY* Who's calling?

Student A: Call your friend David to tell him this:

> There's a party at Bob's house on Saturday night.
> Bob's address is 414 Maple St., Apt. 202.
> Pick me up at 8:00 P.M.

Student B: Someone calls for your brother David. He isn't in. Take a message for him.

Change roles and try another role play.

Student A: Someone calls for your sister Carol. She isn't in. Take a message for her.

Student B: Call your friend Carol to tell her this:

> There's no class next Friday afternoon.
> The class is going to a movie at Westwood Theater.
> Meet us in front of the theater at 4:30.

useful expressions
May I speak to … ?
Can I take a message?
I'll give … the message.

96

Appendix C

12 *READING*

Ways to Keep Phone Calls Short

Do you like to talk on the phone?
Do you think that you spend too much time on the phone?

The phone rings. It's a friend who wants to tell you about his or her latest health problem. You hate to be rude and cut your friend off, but what can you do? Time management consultant Stephanie Winston, author of *Stephanie Winston's Best Organizing Tips*, offers this advice:

1. **Don't ask questions like "What's new?"** They give the impression that you have time to chat. After "hello," get right to the heart of the matter.

2. **Time *your* calls intelligently.** If you make a call right before lunch or dinner, or at the end of the workday, people chat less.

3. **Set a time limit.** Start with, "Hi, I've only got a few minutes, but I wanted to talk to you about ...." Or, "Gee, I'd love to talk more, but I only have a couple of minutes before I have to run errands."

4. **Jump on a pause.** Even the most talkative caller has to pause now and then. Quickly say, "It has been great talking with you." Then end the conversation.

5. **Forget niceties.** Some people just don't take a hint. Interrupt your caller and say, "I'd like to talk to you longer, but I'm pressed for time. Good-bye." Then hang up. Don't ask for permission to end the conversation.

6. **Find a "partner in crime."** If nothing else works, ask someone in your home to help you. For example, one woman signals her husband, who yells, "Jane, I think the roast is burning!"

7. **Avoid the phone completely.** Use an answering machine to screen calls. If you have an important message for a chatterbox, leave the message when he or she isn't in.

A Read the article. Then look at these sentences. Check (✓) the things you can say to keep phone calls short.

☐ 1. I'm glad you feel better. What can I do for you?
☐ 2. I have to go now. Good-bye.
☐ 3. Hi. How are things?
☐ 4. I need to get off the phone now. There's someone at the door.
☐ 5. So, what else is new?
☐ 6. No, I'm not busy right now.
☐ 7. I'm sorry to call you at dinnertime, but I have just one question.
☐ 8. I only have three minutes before I have to leave.

B *Pair work* Talk about these questions.

1. Which advice have you used sometimes?
2. Which do you think are the three best pieces of advice?
3. What else can you do to keep phone calls short?

97

200

interchange 15 *WHAT ARE YOU GOING TO DO?*

A *Class activity* What are your classmates' plans for the weekend?
Go around the class and find people who are going to do these things.
Ask for further information.

Find someone who is going to . . . next weekend.	Name
go on a date	....
stay out all night	....
go to an amusement park	....
go to a party	....
visit friends out of town	....
compete in a sports event	....
see a play	....
go to a garage sale	....

A: Are you going to an amusement park this weekend?
OR
A: Are you going to go to an amusement park this weekend?
B: Yes, I am, actually.
A: Oh, you are? Who are you going with?
B: . . .

B *Pair work* Compare your information with a partner.

IC-20

Source: Richards, J., J. Hull and S. Proctor. 1997. *New Interchange: Student's book 1.*
Cambridge. Cambridge University Press. Pages 92–97, page IC–20.

Appendix D   Graded activities for the four macroskills

In this appendix you will find sets of activities for the four macroskills, which are graded into seven levels of difficulty. These may be useful in the development of your own learning tasks.

Listening

Level 1

- distinguish between English and other languages
- listen to short aural texts and indicate (e.g. by putting up hand) when core vocabulary items are heard
- identify the number and gender of interlocutors
- comprehend and carry out the following instructions: point to, touch, stand up, sit down, go to _____, pick up, put down
- comprehend requests for personal details (name, age, address)
- comprehend requests for the identification of people and things
- listen to simple descriptions of common objects (e.g. those found in the classroom and/or immediate environment) and identify these non-verbally (e.g. by drawing a picture)
- identify letters of the alphabet and numbers to fifty including ten/teen contrasts
- listen to and identify the time

Level 2

- identify core vocabulary items when encountered in a variety of aural texts
- comprehend and carry out a sequence of two to three instructions
- comprehend requests for details about family and friends
- comprehend requests for identification of people and things
- listen to simple descriptions of actions and scenes and identify these non-verbally (e.g. by finding a picture, numbering pictures in the order in which they described)
- given contextual/pictorial support, can comprehend simple descriptions
- identify ordinal numbers 1–10
- listen to and identify days of the week, months and dates

Level 3

- identify core vocabulary items when encountered in a variety of aural texts
- comprehend and carry out a sequence of four to five instructions
- develop factual discrimination skills by listening to a passage and identifying true/false statements relating to the passage
- comprehend requests for factual information relating to topic areas
- listen to a short aural text and transform the information by presenting it in a different form (e.g. by completing a table or diagram)

Level 4

- identify core vocabulary items when encountered in a variety of aural texts
- develop inferencing skills by listening to a passage and identifying true/false inferences relating to the passage
- comprehend requests for factual and attitudinal information relating to topic areas
- listen to a short aural text and transform the information by presenting it in a different form (e.g. by completing a table or diagram)
- comprehend and carry out a linked set of instructions
- grasp the gist of a short narrative
- identify emotional state of speaker from tone and intonation

Level 5

- identify core vocabulary items when encountered in a variety of aural texts
- develop inferencing skills by listening to a passage and identifying true/false inferences relating to the passage
- comprehend requests for factual and attitudinal information relating to topic areas
- listen to a short aural text and transform the information by presenting it in a different form (e.g. by completing a table or diagram)

Level 6

- identify core vocabulary items when encountered in a variety of aural texts
- develop inferencing skills by listening to a passage and suggesting an appropriate conclusion
- comprehend requests for factual and attitudinal information relating to topic areas
- listen to a short aural text and transform the information by presenting it in a different form (e.g. by completing a table or diagram)
- comprehend a short narrative when events are reported out of sequence

Appendix D

Level 7

- extract detailed information from a text
- grasp the gist of an extended text
- follow an extended set of instructions
- differentiate between fact and opinion
- identify the genre and register of a text
- recognize differences in intonation
- identify relationships between participants in aural interactions
- identify the emotional tone of an utterance
- comprehend the details of short conversations on unfamiliar topics

Speaking and oral interaction

Level 1

- name common objects
- give personal details, such as name, age and address
- memorize and recite songs and rhymes in chorus
- take part in short, contextualized dialogues
- give simple (single clause) descriptions of common objects
- request goods and objects
- make statements of ability about self and others

Level 2

- describe family and friends (e.g. refer to age, relationship, size, weight, hair and eye colouring)
- recite songs and rhymes in chorus and individually
- ask and make statements about the likes of self and others
- spell out words from core vocabulary list, and say words when they are spelled out
- answer questions / give details of simple descriptions following an aural presentation
- request details about the family and friends of others using cue words
- make short (one to two sentence) statements on familiar topics using cue words
- talk about regularly occurring activities
- compute quantities and money in English
- tell the time in hours and half hours

Level 3

- answer questions / give details following an aural presentation
- make short (three to four sentence) statements on familiar topics
- following a model, make a series of linked statements about a picture, map, chart or diagram

- work in pairs / small groups to share information and solve a problem
- tell the time using fractions of an hour
- describe a short sequence of past events using sentence cues
- make complete statements from sentence cues when given appropriate contextual support
- make comparisons between physical objects and entities
- use conversational formulae for greeting and leave-taking

Level 4

- answer questions and give details of descriptions following an aural presentation
- describe a picture related to a specific topic area
- narrate a linked sequence of past events shown in a picture sequence or cartoon strip
- work in groups to solve problems which require making inferences and establishing causality
- give opinions about specified issues and topics
- use conversational and discourse strategies e.g. to change subject, provide additional information, invite another person to speak
- give a sequence of directions
- make requests and offers
- talk about future events

Level 5

- give a short summary of the main points of an aural presentation
- give a detailed description of a picture relating to a familiar scene
- describe a simple process
- describe a linked sequence of actions
- work in groups to solve problems requiring the integration of information from a variety of aural and written sources
- give opinions about specified issues and topics
- use conversational and discourse strategies e.g. of holding the floor, disagreeing, qualifying what has been said

Level 6

- give a detailed summary of the main points and supporting details of an aural presentation
- give a prepared oral presentation on a familiar topic
- give a short aural presentation relating to information presented non-textually (e.g. as a chart, map, diagram or graph)
- describe complex processes with the aid of a diagram
- describe a sequence of events in a variety of tenses

205

- work in groups to solve problems requiring the resolution of conflicting information
- comprehend and convey messages by telephone
- qualify one's opinion through the use of modality
- use appropriate non-verbal behaviour

Level 7

- give an unprepared oral presentation on a familiar topic
- use a range of conversational styles from formal to informal
- work in groups to solve problems involving hypothesizing and relating to abstract topics
- initiate and respond to questions of abstract topics
- use a range of conversational and discourse strategies

Reading

Level 1

- sight read all the words in the core vocabulary list when encountered in context
- read the names of class members
- read the written equivalent of numbers 1–60
- read short contextualized lists, e.g. shopping lists
- decode regular sound–symbol correspondences
- read single-sentence descriptions of familiar objects

Level 2

- sight read all the words in the core vocabulary list when encountered in and out of context
- read short (two to three sentence) passages on familiar topics and answer yes/no and true/false questions relating to factual details
- read the written equivalent of numbers 1–100
- read prices and quantities
- decode consonant clusters
- read sentences which have been mastered orally

Level 3

- read short (three to five sentence) passages and answer yes/no and wh-questions relating to factual detail
- read short (three to five sentence) passages and identify correct inferential statements relating to the passage
- read and interpret information presented as a chart or timetable
- dictate a story to the teacher and then read it

Level 4

- read two to three paragraph story on a familiar topic and select the main idea from a list of alternatives
- arrange scrambled sentences and paragraphs into the correct order
- develop dictionary skills (alphabetical order and indexes)
- follow a linked series of written instructions
- read a short passage and predict what will happen next by selecting from a list of alternatives
- scan a three to five paragraph text for given key words
- identify antecedents of anaphoric reference items

Level 5

- read three to five paragraph text and state the main idea
- scan a five to ten paragraph text for given key words
- identify logical relationships marked by conjunctions in three to five paragraph texts on familiar topics
- scan large texts (e.g. dictionary, telephone book) for specific information
- read a short story on a familiar topic and give a short oral summary

Level 6

- read a five to ten paragraph text on a familiar topic and state the main ideas
- read a five to ten paragraph text and present the key information in a non-textual form (e.g. by completing a table or graph)
- identify logical relationships marked by conjunctions in five to ten paragraph texts on unfamiliar topics
- follow a narrative or description when the ideas and events are presented in sequence
- differentiate between fact and opinion

Level 7

- read a five to ten paragraph text on an unfamiliar topic and state the main ideas and supporting details
- identify unmarked logical relationships in five to ten paragraph texts on unfamiliar topics
- follow a narrative or description when the ideas and events are presented out of sequence
- identify instances of bias in a written text
- understand the underlying purpose/function of text
- differentiate between relevant and irrelevant information

Writing

Level 1

- write letters of the alphabet in upper and lower case
- write numbers 1–60
- write own name and names of other students and family members
- copy legibly words in the core vocabulary list
- copy legibly short messages and lists (e.g. shopping lists)
- complete a short contextualized description of a person or object

Level 2

- write numbers 1–100
- use capital letters and full stops appropriately
- write legibly and accurately words in the core vocabulary list
- write short, familiar sentences when dictated

Level 3

- complete short contextualized description of a person or object
- write short, familiar sentences when dictated
- write words and clauses in legible cursive script
- rewrite scrambled sentences as a coherent paragraph

Level 4

- write short, personal note on a familiar topic to a friend (e.g. a postcard)
- write short (one sentence) answers to comprehension questions
- take a short (single paragraph) dictation from a familiar text
- create a paragraph from individual sentences using cohesion to link sentences

Level 5

- write a short description of a familiar object or scene
- write short (two to three sentence) answers to comprehension questions
- write a single paragraph conclusion to a narrative
- take a short (single paragraph) dictation from an unfamiliar text
- develop fluency through free-writing activities

Level 6

- write a summary in point form / précis of a short aural or written text
- produce a text from data provided in non-text form (e.g. as a table, graph or chart)

– write a single paragraph conclusion to a passage presenting an argument
– take a three to five paragraph dictation from a familiar text

Level 7

– use appropriate punctuation conventions
– write a short essay using paragraphs to indicate main information units
– write quickly without pausing, erasing or correcting as part of the process of drafting or composing
– use pre-writing strategies as a preparation for writing
– use revision strategies to polish one's initial efforts

(This is adapted from an unpublished seven-level syllabus developed by me for an ESL curriculum.)

Appendix E   Common reference levels: self-assessment grid

		A1	A2	B1
U N D E R S T A N D I N G	Listening	I can recognise familiar words and very basic phrases concerning myself, my family and immediate concrete surroundings when people speak slowly and clearly.	I can understand phrases and the highest frequency vocabulary related to areas of most immediate personal relevance (e.g. very basic personal and family information, shopping, local area, employment). I can catch the main point in short, clear, simple messages and announcements.	I can understand the main points of clear standard speech on familiar matters regularly encountered in work, school, leisure, etc. I can understand the main point of many radio or TV programmes on current affairs or topics of personal or professional interest when the delivery is relatively slow and clear.
	Reading	I can understand familiar names, words and very simple sentences, for example on notices and posters or in catalogues.	I can read very short, simple texts. I can find specific, predictable information in simple everyday material such as advertisements, prospectuses, menus and timetables and I can understand short simple personal letters.	I can understand texts that consist mainly of high frequency everyday or job-related language. I can understand the description of events, feelings and wishes in personal letters.
S P E A K I N G	Spoken Interaction	I can interact in a simple way provided the other person is prepared to repeat or rephrase things at a slower rate of speech and help me formulate what I'm trying to say. I can ask and answer simple questions in areas of immediate need or on very familiar topics.	I can communicate in simple and routine tasks requiring a simple and direct exchange of information on familiar topics and activities. I can handle very short social exchanges, even though I can't usually understand enough to keep the conversation going myself.	I can deal with most situations likely to arise whilst travelling in an area where the language is spoken. I can enter unprepared into conversation on topics that are familiar, of personal interest or pertinent to everyday life (e.g. family, hobbies, work, travel and current events).
	Spoken Production	I can use simple phrases and sentences to describe where I live and people I know.	I can use a series of phrases and sentences to describe in simple terms my family and other people, living conditions, my educational background and my present or most recent job.	I can connect phrases in a simple way in order to describe experiences and events, my dreams, hopes and ambitions. I can briefly give reasons and explanations for opinions and plans. I can narrate a story or relate the plot of a book or film and describe my reactions.
W R I T I N G	Writing	I can write a short, simple postcard, for example sending holiday greetings. I can fill in forms with personal details, for example entering my name, nationality and address on a hotel registration form.	I can write short, simple notes and messages relating to matters in areas of immediate need. I can write a very simple personal letter, for example thanking someone for something.	I can write simple connected text on topics which are familiar or of personal interest. I can write personal letters describing experiences and impressions.

Source: Council of Europe. 2001. *Common European Framework of Reference for Languages: Learning, teaching, assessement.* Cambridge: Cambridge University Press. Pages 26–27.

B2	C1	C2
I can understand extended speech and lectures and follow even complex lines of argument provided the topic is reasonably familiar. I can understand most TV news and current affairs programmes. I can understand the majority of films in standard dialect.	I can understand extended speech even when it is not clearly structured and when relationships are only implied and not signalled explicitly. I can understand television programmes and films without too much effort.	I have no difficulty in understanding any kind of spoken language, whether live or broadcast, even when delivered at fast native speed, provided I have some time to get familiar with the accent.
I can read articles and reports concerned with contemporary problems in which the writers adopt particular attitudes or viewpoints. I can understand contemporary literary prose.	I can understand long and complex factual and literary texts, appreciating distinctions of style. I can understand specialised articles and longer technical instructions, even when they do not relate to my field.	I can read with ease virtually all forms of the written language, including abstract, structurally or linguistically complex texts such as manuals, specialised articles and literary works.
I can interact with a degree of fluency and spontaneity that makes regular interaction with native speakers quite possible. I can take an active part in discussion in familiar contexts, accounting for and sustaining my views.	I can express myself fluently and spontaneously without much obvious searching for expressions. I can use language flexibly and effectively for social and professional purposes. I can formulate ideas and opinions with precision and relate my contribution skilfully to those of other speakers.	I can take part effortlessly in any conversation or discussion and have a good familiarity with idiomatic expressions and colloquialisms. I can express myself fluently and convey finer shades of meaning precisely. If I do have a problem I can backtrack and restructure around the difficulty so smoothly that other people are hardly aware of it.
I can present clear, detailed descriptions on a wide range of subjects related to my field of interest. I can explain a viewpoint on a topical issue giving the advantages and disadvantages of various options.	I can present clear, detailed descriptions of complex subjects integrating sub-themes, developing particular points and rounding off with an appropriate conclusion.	I can present a clear, smoothly flowing description or argument in a style appropriate to the context and with an effective logical structure which helps the recipient to notice and remember significant points.
I can write clear, detailed text on a wide range of subjects related to my interests. I can write an essay or report, passing on information or giving reasons in support of or against a particular point of view. I can write letters highlighting the personal significance of events and experiences.	I can express myself in clear, well-structured text, expressing points of view at some length. I can write about complex subjects in a letter, an essay or a report, underlining what I consider to be the salient issues. I can select style appropriate to the reader in mind.	I can write clear, smoothly flowing text in an appropriate style. I can write complex letters, reports or articles which present a case with an effective logical structure which helps the recipient to notice and remember significant points. I can write summaries and reviews of professional or literary works.

Glossary

Acquisition: The social and psychological processes through which an individual develops an ability to communicate through language. A basic distinction is drawn between first and second language acquisition.

Aesthetic macrofunction: The use of language for enjoyment and entertainment.

Analytical syllabus: A syllabus based on the notion that learners can acquire language by processing holistic 'chunks' of language and then analyzing the language into its component parts, rather than having the language broken down for them. Topic and content-based syllabuses are analytic in nature.

Assessment: The process of determining what learners can or cannot do. Curriculum-related assessment attempts to link learning outcomes to instruction.

Audiolingualism: A language teaching method based on the behaviourist notion that learning a language is a process of habit formation.

Authenticity: Text authenticity refers to instances of spoken and written language that were produced in the course of genuine communication. Task authenticity refers to tasks that closely mirror communication in the world outside the classroom.

Background knowledge: The real-world knowledge possessed by individuals about a particular subject.

Bottom-up approach: An approach to teaching, learning and using language based on the processing of small units of language and then proceeding to larger units.

Clarification request: A conversational management strategy used by a listener to check that he or she has correctly comprehended the speaker's last utterance.

> A: Make a right on Fifteenth Street.
> B: Did you say Fiftieth or Fifteenth?

Closed task: A task in which there is only one correct answer.

Communicative activity: A pair or groupwork activity that involves the manipulation of a limited number of structures but which allows for genuine information exchange.

Communicative competence: The ability to deploy linguistic, interpersonal and sociocultural knowledge effectively for communicative purposes.

Communicative language teaching: A philosophical approach to language teaching covering a range of methodological approaches which share a focus on helping learners communicate meaningfully in the target language.

Competency-based instruction: One of a number of approaches to instruction in which the curriculum is couched in terms of sets of learner performance.

Comprehensible input: Messages addressed to the learner that may contain phonological, lexical and grammatical features that are beyond the learner's current processing capacity, but that are understandable due to the surrounding context in which they are uttered.

Comprehensible output: The production of spoken output that is comprehensible to the listener. In L2 situations, signals of incomprehension from the listener may prompt a speaker to rephrase an utterance to make it comprehensible. This process is hypothesized to aid acquisition.

Comprehension: Processes through which an individual makes sense of spoken and written language.

Comprehension check: A conversation strategy used by a speaker to ensure that his or her interlocutor has correctly understood.

> A: You need to thread the string through that hole there – you follow?
> B: Uh-huh.

Confirmation check: A strategy used by a listener to confirm that he or she has correctly understood the speaker.

> A: You need to put the string through here.
> B: Through here?
> A: That's right.

Consciousness-raising: Processes and techniques for making learners aware of salient features of the linguistic system.

Constructivism: A philosophical approach arguing that knowledge is socially constructed rather than having its own independent existence.

Content-based instruction: An approach to language teaching in which the syllabus is organized according to content from other subjects on the curriculum, such as history or geography.

Convergent tasks: Tasks in which learners are meant to converge on a single correct answer.

Creative language use: Use of language in which learners have to use pre-learned words and structures in novel ways.

Curriculum: A very broad concept incorporating the elements and processes involved in planning, implementing and evaluating learning.

Data (see Input data)

Declarative knowledge: Knowledge that can be stated (as opposed to demonstrated). Being able to state a grammatical rule is an example of declarative knowledge.

Deductive learning: An instructional process that begins with a statement of rules and principles and then requires learners to apply these to particular examples and instances.

Developmental hypothesis: This hypothesis suggests that grammatical structures can be placed on a continuum from 'early acquired' to 'late acquired', and that this developmental sequence cannot be altered by instruction.

Dialogue: A controlled conversation between two or more participants designed to illustrate and practise one or more language points (these may be grammatical, functional, lexical or phonological).

Divergent tasks: Tasks that encourage a range of possible responses and not a single correct answer (as is the case with convergent tasks).

Evaluation: Processes and procedures for gathering information about a program or curriculum for purposes of improvement.

Exercise (see Language exercise)

Experiential learning: In experiential learning, learners' immediate, personal experiences are taken as the point of departure for the learning process.

First language: An individual's native tongue.

Focus on form: An approach to instruction which provides a systematic focus on language systems (principally, but not exclusively, the grammatical system) within a communicative context. Some researchers, for example Long, argue that this focus should be incidental, and appropriately timed.

Focused tasks: Tasks that are designed to stimulate the production of particular linguistic forms.

Functional syllabus: A syllabus organized according to language functions.

Functions: The general purposes for which people use language, for example socializing, asking for directions, returning an unsatisfactory purchase.

Genre: A staged, goal-oriented, socially constructed written or communicative event.

Goals: The broad, general purposes behind a program, course or curriculum.

Grammar: The study of how form, meaning and use work together to create well-formed sentences.

Group work: Tasks, activities and exercises carried out by learners working in small, co-operative groups.

Humanism: A philosophical movement predicated on the importance of interpersonal relationships and the importance of individual development.

Humanistic psychology: A branch of psychology based on humanism.

Inductive learning: A process of deriving principles or rules from instances or examples.

Information gap: Tasks in which there is a mismatch between the information possessed by different learners in a pair or group-work task. In some cases, one student has all the information (a one-way task); in others, each student has his or her own information (a two-way task).

Input data: The aural and written texts through which learners gain access to the language.

Interlanguage: Language produced by learners in the course of acquiring a second language. It often contains its own 'rules' that deviate from the target language, but that are internally consistent.

Interpersonal language: Language used mainly for socializing (in contrast with transactional language, which is language used for obtaining goods and services, and aesthetic language which is used for enjoyment).

Jigsaw tasks: Tasks involving learners working in groups combining different pieces of information to complete the task.

Language exercise: A procedure in which the aim is to give learners controlled practice at some aspect of the linguistic system (this might be phonological, lexical or grammatical).

Learner-centredness: A philosophical approach to instruction in which content and learning procedures are based on data about the learners for whom the course is designed and, where feasible, on data supplied by learners themselves. The term is also used to describe courses in which learners learn through doing.

Learning strategies: The mental and communicative processes that learners deploy in mastering a second language.

Learning style: A learner's general orientation towards learning.

Macroskills: The four skills of listening, speaking, reading and writing.

Meaningful drill: A language drill designed to manipulate a particular structure, but which also requires students to provide meaningful responses (as opposed to a mechanical drill, which can be completed without the student understanding the meaning of what is said).

Method: A set of procedures for classroom action derived from a set of beliefs about the nature of language and learning. The procedures are usually meant to apply uniformly to all learners regardless of their needs, interests or proficiency level.

Methodology: The subcomponent of the curriculum concerned with selecting, sequencing and justifying learning experiences, as well as the study of the theoretical and empirical bases of such procedures.

Morpheme: The smallest meaningful unit into which a language can be analyzed.

Natural approach: A language teaching method purporting to be based on the principles underlying first language acquisition.

Natural order hypothesis: An hypothesis that grammatical items will be acquired in a predetermined order that cannot be changed by instruction. (See also Developmental hypothesis.)

Needs analysis: Sets of procedures for determining language content and teaching procedures for specified groups of learners.

Negotiation of meaning: The interactional work done by participants in a conversation to ensure mutual understanding. (See also comprehension check, confirmation check, clarification request.)

Notions: General concepts expressed through language, such as time, duration and quantity.

Notional syllabuses: A syllabus arranged according to sets of notions.

Objective (see performance objective).

Open task: A task in which there is no single correct answer.

Opinion-gap tasks: Tasks involving identifying and articulating personal attitudes, feelings or opinions.

Pedagogical grammar: A grammar designed for teaching purposes.

Performance-based approaches: Approaches to pedagogy in which content is specified in terms of observable language performance.

Performance objective: A formal statement of what learners will be able to do (as opposed, for example, to what they will know) at the end of a course of instruction. Formal objectives contain three elements: a task element setting out what learners will do, a conditions element setting out the circumstances under which the task will be performed, and a standards element articulating how well the learner is to perform.

Pragmatics: The study of how individuals use language to achieve particular communicative ends.

Procedural knowledge: Knowledge of how to use language to get things done. Procedural knowledge manifests itself as skills, being a matter of 'knowing how' rather than 'knowing that'.

Procedures: The part of a task specifying what operations learners will perform.

Productive skills: This term is used to refer to speaking and writing.

Proficiency: General language ability.

Psycholinguistics: The study of the mental processes and mechanisms underlying language acquisition and use.

Realia: Items from the world outside the classroom used in language teaching.

Reasoning-gap tasks: Tasks requiring learners to derive new information from given information through cognitive processes such as inferencing, deducing and practical reasoning.

Receptive skills: This term is used to refer to listening and reading.

Reproductive language: Language produced by learners in imitation of models provided by a teacher or by pedagogical materials.

Roles: The social and psychological personas adopted by or imposed upon teachers and learners in the classroom.

Rote learning: Learning through repetition with minimal attention to meaning.

Schema theory: A theory based on the notion that mental frameworks created from past experience guide learning and action.

Second language acquisition: Processes underlying the development of a second and subsequent languages.

Settings: The situations in which learning takes place.

Sociolinguistics: The interpersonal and social processes mediating language learning and use.

Strategies (see Learning strategies)

Syllabus: The subcomponent of a curriculum that specifies and sequences language and experiential content.

Syllabus design: The art and craft of selecting, sequencing and integrating language content.

Syntax: The study of the rules that govern the formation of grammatical structures.

Synthetic syllabus: A syllabus based on the listing of discrete phonological, lexical, grammatical and functional elements.

Systemic–functional linguistics: A theory of language that attempts to establish formal relationships between grammar, meaning and use.

Task: A communicative event having a non-linguistic outcome.

Task-based language teaching: An approach to language teaching organized around tasks rather than language structures.

Teachability / learnability hypothesis: According to this hypothesis, grammatical structures will be acquired, and should be taught, in an order that mirrors difficulty as determined by the processing demands made on the learner's working memory. The order of items determined by processing complexity will differ from the order determined by grammatical complexity. For example, third person 's' is simple from the perspective of grammatical description, but complex in processing terms.

Top-down processing: The use of background knowledge and knowledge of the world to make sense of spoken and written language.

Topic-based instruction: An approach to instruction based on experiential topics.

Unfocused tasks: Tasks that are not intended to elicit a particular grammatical structure.

Transactional language: Language used to obtain goods and services. This use of language contrasts with interpersonal language.

Author index

Subject index

Subject index

affective 61
cognitive 59–60
creative 61
interpersonal 60–61
learner roles 65
and reading 61–63
Syllabus 216
Syllabus design
    analytical approaches 10–12, 212
    definition of 216
    considerations in TBLT 25–31
    process approaches 8
    synthetic approaches 10–12, 216
Systemic-functional linguistics 216
Syntax 216

Task
    versus activity 24
    assessment of 138–164
    -based language teaching 216
    versus exercise 23
    chaining 125–128
    closed 212
    cognitive demand features 88–90
    components 40–73
    continuity 125–128
    convergent 213
    criteria for evaluating 169–170, 173–175
    definitions 1–4, 216
    difficulty 85–90, 171–172
    divergent 214

dependency 35–36
examples of 20–21, 23, 34, 31, 55, 57,
    95, 96, 100–101, 105–105, 122, 126,
    129–131, 133, 134, 135, 144, 145–146,
    155, 187–194, 195–201
features 84–85
focused versus unfocused 94–98, 214,
    217
framework 19–25
versus functions 29–30
open 215
opinion-gap 215
pedagogical 2, 19–21
pedagogical sequence for 31–35
principles for TBLT 35–38
production (for assessment) 154–154
real-word 2, 53
reasoning-gap 216
research 76–91, 93–111
target - *see* real-world
types 56–64, 102–103
Teachability / learnability hypothesis 216
Teacher
    -created tasks 175–177
    education 166–177
    roles 64–65, 68–70
Top-down processing 217 *see also* Schema
    theory
Topic-based / theme-based instruction 131,
    217
Transactional language 217